farmers' market
round-the-seasons cookbook

through-the-year guide to fresh and natural organic
cooking with over 100 delicious recipes

ysanne spevack

southwater

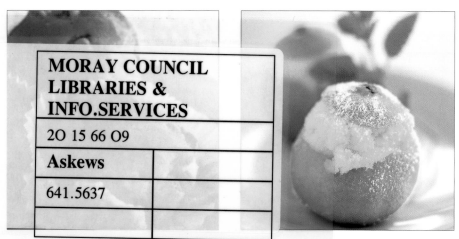

This edition is published by Southwater

Southwater is an imprint of Anness Publishing Ltd
Hermes House, 88–89 Blackfriars Road, London SE1 8HA
tel. 020 7401 2077; fax 020 7633 9499
www.southwaterbooks.com; info@anness.com

© Anness Publishing Ltd 2004

UK agent: The Manning Partnership Ltd
6 The Old Dairy, Melcombe Road, Bath BA2 3LR
tel. 01225 478444; fax 01225 478440
sales@manning-partnership.co.uk

UK distributor: Grantham Book Services Ltd
Isaac Newton Way, Alma Park Industrial Estate,
Grantham, Lincs NG31 9SD
tel. 01476 541080; fax 01476 541061; orders@gbs.tbs-ltd.co.uk

North American agent/distributor: National Book Network
4501 Forbes Boulevard, Suite 200, Lanham, MD 20706
tel. 301 459 3366; fax 301 429 5746; www.nbnbooks.com

Australian agent/distributor: Pan Macmillan Australia
Level 18, St Martins Tower, 31 Market St, Sydney, NSW 2000
tel. 1300 135 113; fax 1300 135 103
customer.service@macmillan.com.au

New Zealand agent/distributor: David Bateman Ltd
30 Tarndale Grove, Off Bush Road, Albany, Auckland
tel. (09) 415 7664; fax (09) 415 8892

A CIP catalogue record for this book is available
from the British Library.

Publisher: Joanna Lorenz
Editors: Joy Wotton and Elizabeth Woodland
Jacket Design: Balley Design Associates
Photographers: Peter Anderson and Simon Smith
Production Controller: Darren Price

Previously published as part of a larger volume,
The Organic Cookbook

10 9 8 7 6 5 4 3 2 1

NOTES
Bracketed terms are for American readers. For all recipes,
quantities are given in both metric and imperial measures and,
where appropriate, measures are also given in standard cups
and spoons. Follow one set, but not a mixture because they
are not interchangeable. Standard spoon and cup measures
are level. 1 tsp = 5ml, 1 tbsp = 15ml, 1 cup = 250ml/8fl oz.
Australian standard tablespoons are 20ml. Australian readers
should use 3 tsp in place of 1 tbsp for measuring small
quantities of gelatine, cornflour, salt etc. Medium (US large)
eggs are used unless otherwise stated.

farmers' market
round-the-seasons cookbook

CONTENTS

INTRODUCTION

All organic food is good for you. It also tastes better. Fresh organic produce contains more vitamins, minerals, enzymes and other micronutrients than intensively farmed agrochemical produce.

Organic food is the fastest growing sector of the entire food industry. Step into any supermarket or shopping mall, and you will see an impressive array of delicious and colourful organic produce. Organic meat, poultry and dairy produce are of excellent quality and usually lower in saturated fat than non-organic. Organic fruit and vegetables are full of juice and flavour, and today there are many different varieties to try.

Mainstream shops are often the first point of contact for shoppers unfamiliar with organic food, but having experienced the superior flavours and learned of the undeniable health benefits, many people go on to investigate box schemes, farmers' markets featuring organic produce and small, local organic suppliers.

Below: Organic fruit and vegetables on sale at a local farmers' market are really fresh and full of goodness.

Improved Health

There are dozens – many would say hundreds – of excellent reasons for choosing the organic option. Apart from benefits to the individual in terms of health, avoidance of chemicals and the sheer enjoyment of eating food that is full of flavour, there are environmental issues to consider, as well as moral questions such as animal welfare, the health of farm workers and fair trade.

Vitamins and Minerals The reason that fresh organic produce contains more vitamins and minerals than the agrochemical equivalent is largely due to the method of cultivation. Organic fruits and vegetables are not sprayed with artificial fertilizers, but are allowed to grow and ripen more naturally in richer soil, obtaining the maximum variety of micronutrients.

Phytonutrients All fresh produce contains phytonutrients or naturally occurring chemical compounds, but organic produce contains more than its non-organic equivalent. They are found in fresh fruit and vegetables and help to fight disease and promote good health. More research is needed to pinpoint the

Above: Eating an organic diet before conception and during pregnancy will help rid the body of toxins.

precise benefits of all these compounds, but much is already known. Glucosinolates in cabbage, broccoli, cauliflower and Brussels sprouts help prevent cancer. Flavonoids are powerful antioxidants found in onions and garlic. Regular consumption of onions and garlic significantly reduces the risk of heart disease and the spread of cancer.

Fats Hydrogenated fats are oils that have had hydrogen added to them so that they become solid or semi-solid at room temperature. Nutritionists universally agree that they are a major cofactor in heart disease, cancer, diabetes and obesity. The surest way to remove hydrogenated fats from your diet is to go organic. Organic food regulations throughout the world prohibit the use of hydrogenated fats. Saturated fat is present in organic beef as well as in intensively reared beef, but the percentage is likely to be lower.

The Organic Movement

Interest in organic food and farming is at an all-time high. This is partly because people are better informed about nutrition, more concerned about the environment and more cautious about the short- and long-term effects of diet on health than at any time in the past, but there are also more fundamental reasons, such as flavour. To put it simply, we appreciate good food. This generation is more widely travelled than

Right: Organic cattle are less susceptible to disease because they are always free range and have access to the outdoors.

any previous one, and is discovering exotic cuisines and exciting new tastes from all over the world. People eat out more often, and are more adventurous when cooking at home. As palates become increasingly sophisticated, we demand more from the ingredients that make up our meals, so it is hardly surprising that we increasingly favour organic food.

Farming Organic

Food labelled organic has been produced according to strict and rigidly regulated guidelines. Organic farm animals and poultry are treated with respect, without recourse to artificial hormones, antibiotics or routine drug therapies. Inhumane practices such as battery farming are banned. Dairy cows raised organically have, on average, 50 per cent more room in their barns than non-organic cows, and unlike the latter, they are always provided with bedding.

Organic farming is the cultivation of crops and rearing of livestock with natural soil fertility at the heart of the system. Organic farmers believe that by working hard to maintain and encourage good soil structure on their land, the crops and livestock grown and bred there will flourish. Produce is grown without the routine use of pesticides or artificial fertilizers, and animals are reared without being treated with growth promoters or unnecessarily dosed with antibiotics.

Modern organic farming is highly scientific and makes considerable use of technology. Yields from organic and agrochemical farms are now almost identical, and organic yields continue to grow as a result of continued research into intensive organic agriculture. Organic farmers also benefit from access to much wider seed banks than those customarily used by agrochemical farmers, so they can select the best varieties of crops for their climate and terrain.

Organic Livestock

Animal welfare is a fundamental principle of organic livestock, poultry and dairy farming. Organic animals are always free range. Because they have access to the outdoors, they are less susceptible to disease and, although farmers will take appropriate action if an animal becomes unwell, there is no need for the routine administration of antibiotics that is standard preventative practice on agrochemical farms. Organic farmers often use such complementary medicines as homeopathic treatments to cure a sick animal, and they inject antibiotics only as a last resort, when other treatments have failed.

Organic farmers are not allowed to use hormones to encourage animal growth or increase milk production. In countries where growth hormones such as BST (bovine somatotropin) are administered, dairy cows often suffer intense pain from unnaturally swollen udders. Their milk contains the same hormones, increasing the consumer's risk of multi-generational cancers and hormone disruption disorders.

Fish

Organic fish, whether wild or farmed, should come from sustainable fisheries and farms and be caught using fishing practices that protect the environment.

Wild Fish Logic dictates that all wild fish are organic, since they swim and eat where they will. However, pollution, insensitive fishing methods and proximity to major shipping lanes all have a detrimental effect on wild fish stocks, and there is no standard for organics in wild fish. The Marine Stewardship Council is an international organization offering an accreditation scheme for sustainable wild fisheries.

Farmed Fish The conditions under which fish are farmed vary widely. For farmed fish to be labelled organic they must have adequate room to move, be allowed to grow and develop naturally, and be given organic feed. This is not the case on many agrochemical fish farms, where fish populations can be so high and intensive that infestation and disease are commonplace and chemical pesticides must be used liberally to control them.

The Balanced Diet

A wholesome, organic diet provides balanced nutrition, including a healthy range of vitamins, minerals and phytonutrients. This is an important consideration in a world where many people opt for convenience foods that are often high in fat and sugar and offer little in terms of nutrition. There is a direct correlation between over-consumption malnutrition trends in industrialized nations and eating non-organic food.

Improved Immunity There is evidence to suggest that people who eat organic food build up a stronger immunity to disease than those who consistently eat food that is laden with chemicals. The consumption of over-processed, non-organic junk food puts a strain on immune systems already compromised by living in a polluted world, by forcing the liver and kidneys to work harder to remove the toxins they frequently contain.

Increased Fertility Studies appear to support a link between organic diets and increased fertility in men. Because a balanced organic diet is more nutritionally sound and contains fewer chemicals or artificial hormones than a non-organic diet it is bound to offer the best option for men – and women – wanting to support their sexual health and improve their chances of conceiving.

Above: Modern organic farmers grow crops and raise livestock without the aid of potentially damaging agrochemicals, pesticides and artificial fertilizers.

Avoiding the Chemical Cocktail

The average adult living in one of the industrialized nations has between 300 and 500 agrochemical pesticides in his or her body at any one time. Pesticides can remain stored in body fat for many years. No long-term studies have truly evaluated the damage to our health these chemicals pose, but there is evidence to suggest they exacerbate chronic conditions and seriously undermine health.

Children are particularly susceptible to agrochemical toxins. They have a higher intake of food than adults in relation to their body weight, and their bodies are less efficient at eliminating toxins. Breast milk from mothers whose diets are not organic generally contains concentrations of pesticides. These have been shown to adversely affect brain development in babies. Ideally, a woman planning to conceive a child should adopt an organic diet at least one year before falling pregnant. This gives her

Left: Fresh tomatoes grown in an organic vegetable garden are an excellent option for the health-conscious consumer.

body time to detoxify, helping to create a healthier environment for the foetus to grow in and then purer breast milk for the baby once it has been born.

Artificial Additives Seven thousand artificial additives are permitted to be used in conventional food. Only seven of these are allowed to be used in processed organic food. Although some artificial additives are absolutely harmless, many undermine our health.

Antibiotics and Hormones

Intensively reared livestock are routinely fed and injected with antibiotics to keep them healthy. These substances pass into their meat. People who eat this meat develop reduced immunity through over-exposure to antibiotics. Hormones and endocrine disrupting chemicals (EDCs) also pose a threat to health. Five out of the twelve most commonly used pesticides in the world are known to be EDCs, and these are known to affect the delicate balance of human hormones.

Food Safety

All organic animals that are naturally vegetarian are fed only vegetarian food. This was a huge benefit during the UK's BSE (Bovine Spongiform Encephalopathy) crisis. BSE was caused and spread because cows were fed contaminated food, which was itself animal in origin. All organic farms in the UK are completely BSE-free because organic cows are always fed food that is 100 per cent vegetarian.

Organic meat and dairy produce is free from genetically modified organisms or GMOs because all food for organic animals must be GMO-free by law. The diet of organic animals is also solvent free. This may seem obvious until it is considered that non-organic animals regularly eat food contaminated with solvents. Non-organic cooking oil is usually produced by soaking oil-rich vegetable matter in solvents. The oil is then extracted from the liquid, and the remaining solid matter is used for animal feed. Solvent-extracted animal feed is banned from organic farms.

Natural Flavours

During the year 2000, 43 per cent of consumers who bought organic food in Britain declared that they did so because they thought it tasted better than non-organic food. Tastes vary from person to person, but there are sound reasons why organic food tastes better.

The slower growth rates of organic crops allow more time for flavour and nutrients to develop naturally. Although much organic produce is currently grown a long way from the point of sale, it is best to buy it fresh from local producers. The range of organic foods may not be as great as that of non-organic produce, but the pleasure of enjoying seasonal treats such as strawberries in summer at the same time as helping to sustain the environment provides a more than adequate compensation.

Above: Organic cheeses are made from organic milk and offer all the environmental, humanitarian and healthy-eating benefits of other organic dairy products.

Below: Livestock, such as sheep, raised on organic farms enjoy a healthy stress-free lifestyle.

SPRING

As the days start to get a little longer and the weather gets warmer, the fresh organic ingredients traditionally associated with this time of year – such as tender young vegetables and new season lamb – start to appear in the shops and farmers' markets.

The season's vegetables require little cooking to bring out their sweet flavour: try asparagus with a tangy lemon sauce, sweet young carrots and leeks, or escalopes of chicken with new potatoes. Brightly coloured spring vegetables also look and taste good when served with pasta, or when added to soups.

Light fish dishes are a popular choice now after long, dark winter days – Salmon Fish Cakes, or Fillets of Sea Bream in Filo Pastry, served simply with spring vegetables, are a real treat. And this is the time of year to enjoy organic lamb, in dishes such as Herb-crusted Rack of Lamb with Puy Lentils, and Lamb Burgers with Red Onion and Tomato Relish. For dessert, nothing tastes better than tender spring rhubarb served with ginger ice cream, or made into a meringue pie.

CHICKEN, AVOCADO and SPRING ONION SOUP

Organic avocados ripen naturally over a longer period of time than non-organic, producing really rich-flavoured fruit. Combined here with chicken and spring onions they add a creaminess to this delicious soup.

SERVES SIX

1.5 litres/2½ pints/6¼ cups chicken stock
½ fresh chilli, seeded
2 skinless, boneless chicken breast fillets
1 avocado
4 spring onions (scallions), finely sliced
400g/14oz can chickpeas, drained
sea salt and freshly ground black pepper

1 Pour the chicken stock into a large pan and add the chilli. Bring to the boil, add the whole chicken breast fillets, then lower the heat and simmer for about 10 minutes, or until the chicken is cooked.

COOK'S TIP
Handle chillies with care as they can irritate the skin and eyes. It is advisable to wear rubber gloves when preparing them.

2 Remove the pan from the heat and lift out the chicken breasts with a slotted spoon. Leave to cool a little, then, using two forks, shred the chicken into small pieces. Set the shredded chicken aside.

3 Pour the chicken stock into a food processor or blender and add the chilli. Process the mixture until smooth, then return to the pan.

4 Cut the avocado in half, remove the skin and stone (pit), then slice the flesh into 2cm/¾in pieces. Add it to the stock, with the spring onions and chickpeas.

5 Return the shredded chicken to the pan, with salt and pepper to taste, and heat gently. When the soup is heated through, spoon into warmed bowls and serve.

PASTA and CHICKPEA SOUP

A simple, country-style soup. The shapes of the pasta and the beans complement one another beautifully. Look out for really large pasta shells, which you can find in farmers' markets and good organic stores.

SERVES FOUR TO SIX

1 onion
2 carrots
2 celery sticks
60ml/4 tbsp olive oil
400g/14oz can chickpeas, rinsed
    and drained
200g/7oz can cannellini beans,
    rinsed and drained
150ml/¼ pint/⅔ cup passata (bottled
    strained tomatoes)
120ml/4fl oz/½ cup water
1.5 litres/2½ pints/6¼ cups chicken stock
2 fresh or dried rosemary sprigs
200g/7oz dried giant conchiglie
sea salt and ground black pepper
freshly grated Parmesan cheese or
    premium Italian-style vegetarian
    cheese, to serve

1 Chop the onion, carrots and celery sticks finely, either in a food processor or by hand.

2 Heat the olive oil in a large pan, add the chopped vegetable mixture and cook over a low heat, stirring frequently, for 5 minutes, or until the vegetables are just beginning to soften.

3 Add the chickpeas and cannellini beans, stir well to mix, then cook for 5 minutes. Stir in the passata and water, then cook, stirring, for 2–3 minutes.

4 Add 475ml/16fl oz/2 cups of the stock and one of the rosemary sprigs. Bring to the boil, cover, then simmer gently, stirring occasionally, for 1 hour.

5 Pour in the remaining stock, add the pasta and bring to boil, stirring. Lower the heat slightly and simmer, stirring frequently, until the pasta is *al dente*: 7–8 minutes or according to the instructions on the packet.

6 When the pasta is cooked, taste the soup for seasoning. Remove the rosemary and serve the soup hot in warmed bowls, topped with grated cheese and a few rosemary leaves from the rosemary sprig.

COOK'S TIP
Organic passata is a must for this recipe as most non-organic tomato products contain genetically modified tomatoes.

TAPENADE with QUAIL'S EGGS and CRUDITÉS

This olive-based spread or dip makes a sociable start to a meal. Serve the tapenade with hard-boiled quail's eggs or small organic hen's eggs and a selection of mixed spring vegetable crudités and let everyone help themselves.

SERVES SIX

225g/8oz/2 cups pitted black olives
2 large garlic cloves, peeled
15ml/1 tbsp salted capers, rinsed
6 canned or bottled anchovy
    fillets, drained
50g/2oz good-quality canned tuna
5–10ml/1–2 tsp Cognac (optional)
5ml/1 tsp chopped fresh thyme
30ml/2 tbsp chopped fresh parsley
30–60ml/2–4 tbsp extra virgin olive oil
a dash of lemon juice
30ml/2 tbsp crème fraîche or
    fromage frais (optional)
12–18 quail's eggs
ground black pepper

For the crudités
bunch of spring onions (scallions),
    halved if large
bunch of radishes, trimmed
bunch of baby fennel, trimmed and halved
    if large, or 1 large fennel bulb, cut into
    thin wedges

To serve
French bread
unsalted (sweet) butter or olive oil and
    sea salt to dip

1 Process the olives, garlic cloves, capers, anchovies and tuna in a food processor or blender. Transfer to a mixing bowl and stir in the Cognac, if using, the thyme, parsley and enough olive oil to make a paste. Season to taste with pepper and a dash of lemon juice. Stir in the crème fraîche or fromage frais, if using, and transfer to a serving bowl.

2 Place the quail's eggs in a pan of cold water and bring to the boil. Cook for only 2 minutes, then immediately drain and plunge the eggs into iced water to stop them from cooking any further and to help make them easier to shell.

3 When the eggs are cold, carefully part-shell them.

4 Serve the tapenade with the eggs and crudités and offer French bread, unsalted butter or oil and sea salt to accompany them.

COOK'S TIPS
• Crème fraîche or fromage frais softens the distinctive flavour of the olives for a milder tapenade.
• In Provence, where tapenade comes from, it is traditional to serve it with crudités of celery, fennel and tomato.
• Tapenade is also delicious spread on toast and served with pre-dinner drinks.

OYSTERS ROCKEFELLER

This is the perfect dish for those who prefer to eat their oysters lightly cooked. As a cheaper alternative, for those who are not "as rich as Rockefeller", give mussels or clams the same treatment; they will also taste delicious.

SERVES SIX

450g/1lb/3 cups coarse sea salt,
　　plus extra to serve
24 oysters, opened
115g/4oz/½ cup butter or
　　non-hydrogenated margarine
2 shallots, finely chopped
500g/1¼lb spinach leaves, finely chopped
60ml/4 tbsp chopped fresh parsley
60ml/4 tbsp chopped celery leaves
90ml/6 tbsp fresh white or wholemeal
　　(whole-wheat) breadcrumbs
10–20ml/2–4 tsp vodka
cayenne pepper
sea salt and ground black pepper
lemon wedges, to serve

COOK'S TIP

If you prefer a smoother stuffing, whizz it to a paste in a food processor or blender at the end of step 3.

1 Preheat the oven to 220°C/425°F/ Gas 7. Make a bed of coarse salt on two large baking sheets. Set the oysters in the half-shell in the bed of salt to keep them steady. Set aside.

2 Melt the butter or margarine in a frying pan. Add the chopped shallots and cook them over a low heat for 2–3 minutes until they are softened. Stir in the spinach and let it wilt.

3 Add the parsley, celery leaves and breadcrumbs to the pan and fry gently for 5 minutes. Season with salt, pepper and cayenne pepper.

4 Divide the stuffing among the oysters. Drizzle a few drops of vodka over each oyster, then bake for about 5 minutes until bubbling and golden brown. Serve on a heated platter on a shallow salt bed with lemon wedges.

LEEK and MUSSEL TARTLETS

Wild mussels are easily harvested and are simply gathered off rocks in shallow water by hand. Serve these vividly coloured little tarts as a first course, with a few salad leaves, such as watercress, rocket and frisée.

3 Preheat the oven to 190°C/375°F/ Gas 5. Roll out the pastry and line six 10cm/4in tartlet tins (quiche pans). Prick the bases and line the sides with foil. Bake for 10 minutes. Remove the foil and bake for 5–8 minutes. Reduce the temperature to 180°C/350°F/Gas 4.

4 Soak the saffron in 15ml/1 tbsp hot water for 10 minutes. Fry the leeks in the oil in a pan over a medium heat for 6–8 minutes. Add the peppers and cook for 2 minutes.

SERVES SIX

large pinch of saffron threads
2 large leeks, sliced
30ml/2 tbsp olive oil
2 large yellow (bell) peppers, halved, seeded, grilled (broiled), peeled and cut into strips
900g/2lb mussels
2 large eggs
300ml/½ pint/1¼ cups single (light) cream or soya cream
30ml/2 tbsp finely chopped fresh parsley
sea salt and ground black pepper
salad leaves, to serve

For the pastry
225g/8oz/2 cups plain (all-purpose) flour
115g/4oz/½ cup chilled butter, diced
45–60ml/3–4 tbsp chilled water

1 To make the pastry, sift the flour into a mixing bowl and add the butter. Rub the butter in with your fingertips until the mixture resembles fine breadcrumbs.

2 Sprinkle 45ml/3 tbsp of the water over and mix with a round-bladed knife until the mixture comes together and a soft dough is formed. Add more water if necessary. Wrap the dough in clear film (plastic wrap) and chill for 30 minutes.

COOK'S TIP

Use soya cream instead of the single cream and soya margarine instead of butter for a non-dairy option.

5 Bring 2.5cm/1in depth of water to the boil in a large pan and add 10ml/2 tsp salt. Scrub the mussels and remove the beards. Discard any mussels that stay open when tapped, then throw the rest into the pan. Cover and cook over a high heat, shaking the pan occasionally, for 3–4 minutes, or until the mussels open. Discard any unopened mussels. Shell the remainder.

6 Beat the eggs, cream and saffron liquid together. Season with salt and pepper and whisk in the parsley. Arrange the leeks, peppers and mussels in the cases, add the egg mixture and bake for 20–25 minutes. Serve with salad leaves.

DEEP-FRIED TOFU BALLS

Tofu is a wonderfully healthy and versatile ingredient and is flavoured to perfection in this Japanese dish, known as hiryozu, which means flying dragon's head. The tangy lime sauce provides a lovely contrast to the savoury tofu balls.

SERVES FOUR

2 × 285g/10¼oz packets firm tofu
20g/¾oz carrot, peeled
40g/1½oz green beans
2 large (US extra large) eggs, beaten
30ml/2 tbsp sake
10ml/2 tsp mirin
5ml/1 tsp sea salt
10ml/2 tsp shoyu
pinch of unrefined caster (superfine) sugar
     or rapadura
sunflower oil, for deep-frying

For the lime sauce
45ml/3 tbsp shoyu
juice of ½ lime
5ml/1 tsp rice vinegar or mirin

To garnish
300g/11oz mooli (daikon), peeled
2 dried red chillies, halved and seeded
4 chives, finely chopped

1 Drain the tofu and wrap in a dishtowel or kitchen paper. Set a chopping board on top and leave for 2 hours, or until it loses most of its liquid.

2 Cut the mooli for the garnish into about 4cm/1½in thick slices. Make 3–4 small holes in each slice with a skewer or chopstick and insert chilli pieces into the holes. Leave for 15 minutes, then grate the daikon and chilli finely.

3 To make the tofu balls, chop the carrot finely. Trim and cut the beans into 5mm/¼in lengths. Cook both vegetables for 1 minute in boiling water.

4 In a food processor, blend the tofu, eggs, sake, mirin, salt, shoyu and sugar until smooth. Transfer to a bowl and mix in the carrot and beans.

5 Fill a wok or pan with oil 4cm/1½in deep, and heat to 185°C/365°F.

6 Soak a piece of kitchen paper with a little vegetable oil, and lightly moisten your hands with it. Scoop 40ml/2½ tbsp of the mixture in one hand and shape into a ball between your hands.

7 Carefully slide the ball into the oil and deep-fry until crisp and golden brown. Drain on kitchen paper. Repeat with the remaining mixture.

8 Arrange the tofu balls on a plate and sprinkle with chives. Put 30ml/2 tbsp grated mooli in each of four bowls. Mix the lime sauce ingredients in a small serving bowl. Serve the hot tofu balls with the lime sauce to be mixed with grated daikon by each guest.

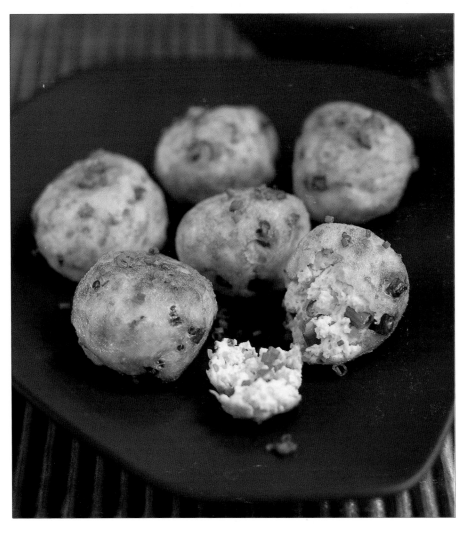

ASPARAGUS with LEMON SAUCE

This is a good spring dish as the asparagus gives the immune system a kick start to help detoxify after winter. The sauce has a light, fresh taste and brings out the best in asparagus.

SERVES FOUR AS A FIRST COURSE

675g/1½lb asparagus, tough ends removed, and tied in a bundle
15ml/1 tbsp cornflour (cornstarch)
10ml/2 tsp unrefined sugar or rapadura
2 egg yolks
juice of 1½ lemons
sea salt

COOK'S TIP
Use tiny asparagus spears for an elegant appetizer for a special dinner party.

1 Cook the bundle of asparagus in boiling salted water for 7–10 minutes.

2 Drain the asparagus well (reserving 200ml/7fl oz/scant 1 cup of the cooking liquid) and arrange the spears attractively in a serving dish. Set aside.

3 Blend the cornflour with the cooled, reserved cooking liquid and place in a small pan. Bring to the boil, stirring all the time with a wooden spoon, then cook over a gentle heat until the sauce thickens slightly. Stir in the sugar, then remove the pan from the heat and allow to cool slightly.

4 Beat the egg yolks thoroughly with the lemon juice and stir gradually into the cooled sauce. Cook the sauce over a very low heat, stirring all the time, until it thickens. Be careful not to overheat the sauce or it may curdle. Once the sauce has thickened, remove the pan from the heat and continue stirring for 1 minute. Season with salt or sugar if necessary. Allow the sauce to cool slightly.

5 Stir the cooled lemon sauce, then pour a little over the cooked asparagus. Cover and chill for at least 2 hours before serving accompanied by the rest of the lemon sauce.

BRAISED LEEKS with CARROTS

Sweet carrots and leeks go well together and are delicious finished with a little chopped mint or chervil. This is an easy accompaniment to roast lamb for a spring Sunday lunch.

4 Add seasoning, the wine and half the chopped herb. Heat until simmering, then cover and cook gently for 5–8 minutes until the leeks are tender, but not collapsed.

5 Uncover the leeks and turn them in the buttery juices. Increase the heat slightly, then boil the liquid rapidly until reduced to a few tablespoons.

6 Add the carrots to the leeks and reheat them gently, then swirl in the remaining butter or oil. Adjust the seasoning, if necessary. Transfer to a warmed serving dish and serve sprinkled with the remaining chopped herb.

VARIATION

Braised leeks in tarragon cream
Cook 900g/2lb leeks in 40g/1½oz/3 tbsp butter or 45ml/3 tbsp olive oil as above. Season, add a pinch of sugar, 45ml/3 tbsp tarragon vinegar, 6 fresh tarragon sprigs and 60ml/4 tbsp white wine. Cover and cook as above. Add 150ml/¼ pint/⅔ cup double (heavy) cream or soya cream and allow to bubble and thicken. Season and sprinkle with chopped fresh tarragon.

SERVES SIX

65g/2½oz/5 tbsp butter or
   75ml/5 tbsp olive oil
675g/1½lb carrots, thickly sliced
2 fresh bay leaves
75ml/5 tbsp water
675g/1½lb leeks, cut into 5cm/
   2in lengths
120ml/4fl oz/½ cup white wine
30ml/2 tbsp chopped fresh mint
   or chervil
sea salt and ground black pepper

1 Heat 25g/1oz/2 tbsp of the butter or 30ml/2 tbsp of oil in a pan and cook the carrots gently for 4–5 minutes.

2 Add the bay leaves, seasoning and the water to the pan. Bring to the boil, cover lightly and cook for 10–15 minutes until the carrots are tender. Uncover, then boil the cooking juices until they have all evaporated, leaving the carrots moist and glazed.

3 Meanwhile, heat another 25g/1oz/ 2 tbsp of the remaining butter or 30ml/2 tbsp of oil in a deep frying pan or wide pan that will take the sliced leeks in a single layer. Add the leeks and fry them very gently in the melted butter over a medium to low heat for 4–5 minutes, without allowing them to turn brown.

GARGANELLI with SPRING VEGETABLES

Fresh, brightly coloured spring vegetables both look and taste good when served with pasta. A light sauce of dry white wine, extra virgin olive oil and fresh herbs is used to marry the two together for a delicious flavour.

SERVES FOUR

1 bunch asparagus, about 350g/12oz
4 young carrots
1 bunch spring onions (scallions)
130g/4½oz shelled fresh peas
350g/12oz/3 cups dried garganelli
60ml/4 tbsp dry white wine
90ml/6 tbsp extra virgin olive oil
a few sprigs fresh flat leaf parsley, mint and
    basil, leaves stripped and chopped
sea salt and ground black pepper
freshly grated Parmesan cheese or premium
    Italian-style vegetarian cheese, to serve

1 Trim off and discard the woody part of each asparagus stem, then cut off the tips on the diagonal. Cut the stems on the diagonal into 4cm/1½in pieces. Cut the carrots and spring onions on the diagonal into similar-size pieces.

2 Plunge the carrots, peas, asparagus stems and tips into a large pan of salted boiling water. Bring back to the boil, then reduce the heat and simmer for 8–10 minutes, until tender.

3 Meanwhile, cook the pasta in salted boiling water for 10–12 minutes, or according to the instructions on the packet, until just tender.

4 Drain the asparagus, carrots and peas and return them to the pan. Add the white wine, olive oil and salt and black pepper to taste, then gently toss over a medium to high heat until the wine has reduced and the vegetables glisten with the olive oil.

5 Drain the garganelli and tip it into a warmed large bowl. Add the vegetables, spring onions and sprigs of fresh herbs and toss well. Divide the pasta among four warmed individual plates and serve immediately, with freshly grated cheese.

COOK'S TIP
Garganelli are rolled short pasta shapes made with pasta dough enriched with egg. If you can't get garganelli, use another short shape, such as penne.

PENNE with CREAM and SMOKED SALMON

This modern classic uses just three essential ingredients, which combine together
beautifully to make a quick and easy dish. Accompany with a green salad, ciabatta bread
and sparkling wine for a simple but nutritious and tasty meal.

SERVES FOUR

350g/12oz/3 cups dried penne or
   other pasta tubes
115g/4oz thinly sliced smoked salmon
2–3 fresh thyme sprigs
30ml/2 tbsp extra virgin olive oil
150ml/¼ pint/⅔ cup extra-thick
   single (light) cream or
   soya cream
sea salt and ground black pepper

1 Cook the dried pasta in a large pan of lightly salted boiling water for 10 minutes until it is just tender, or according to the instructions on the packet.

2 Meanwhile, using sharp kitchen scissors, cut the smoked salmon slices into thin strips, about 5mm/¼in wide. Strip the leaves from the thyme sprigs and rinse them thoroughly in cold water.

3 Drain the pasta and return it to the pan. Add the oil and heat gently, then stir in the cream with about one-quarter of the smoked salmon and thyme leaves, then season with pepper. Heat gently for 3–4 minutes, stirring all the time. Check the seasoning. Divide the pasta among four warmed bowls, top with the remaining salmon and thyme leaves and serve immediately.

VARIATION
Although white penne is the traditional pasta to serve with this sauce, it also goes very well with fresh wholemeal penne or ravioli stuffed with spinach and ricotta cheese.

CHICKEN and ASPARAGUS RISOTTO

Use fairly thick asparagus in this classic springtime risotto, as fine spears tend to overcook. The thick ends of the asparagus are full of flavour and they become beautifully tender in the time it takes for the rice to absorb the stock.

SERVES FOUR

75ml/5 tbsp olive oil
1 leek, finely chopped
115g/4oz/1½ cups oyster or brown cap
   (cremini) mushrooms, sliced
3 skinless, boneless chicken breast
   fillets, cubed
350g/12oz asparagus
250g/9oz/1¼ cups risotto rice
900ml/1½ pints/3¾ cups simmering
   chicken stock
sea salt and ground black pepper
fresh Parmesan or premium
   Italian-style vegetarian cheese curls,
   to serve

1 Heat the olive oil in a pan. Add the finely chopped leek and cook gently until softened, but not coloured. Add the sliced mushrooms and cook for 5 minutes. Remove the vegetables from the pan and set aside.

2 Increase the heat and cook the cubes of chicken until golden on all sides. Do this in batches, if necessary, and then return them all to the pan.

3 Meanwhile, discard the woody ends from the asparagus and cut the spears in half. Set the tips aside. Cut the thick ends in half and add them to the pan. Return the leek and mushroom mixture to the pan and stir in the rice.

4 Pour in a ladleful of boiling stock and cook gently, stirring occasionally, until the stock is completely absorbed. Continue adding the stock a ladleful at a time, simmering until it is absorbed, the rice is tender and the chicken is cooked.

COOK'S TIP
To thoroughly remove all the soil from organic leeks, slice in half along their length and rinse under running water.

5 Add the asparagus tips with the last ladleful of boiling stock for the final 5 minutes and continue cooking the risotto very gently until the asparagus is tender. The whole process should take about 25–30 minutes.

6 Season the risotto to taste with salt and freshly ground black pepper and spoon it into individual warm serving bowls. Top each bowl with curls of cheese, and serve.

ESCALOPES of CHICKEN with VEGETABLES

This is a quick and light dish – ideal as the weather starts to warm up and easy meals become the order of the day. Flattening the chicken breasts thins and tenderizes the meat and also speeds up the cooking time.

SERVES FOUR

4 skinless, boneless chicken breast fillets,
    each weighing 175g/6oz
juice of 1 lime
120ml/4fl oz/½ cup olive oil
675g/1½lb mixed small new season
    potatoes, carrots, fennel (sliced
    if large), asparagus and peas
sea salt and ground black pepper
sprigs of fresh flat leaf parsley, to garnish

For the tomato mayonnaise
150ml/¼ pint/⅔ cup mayonnaise
15ml/1 tbsp sun-dried tomato
    purée (paste)

1 Lay the chicken fillets between sheets of clear film (plastic wrap) or baking parchment and use a rolling pin to beat them until they are evenly thin. Season the chicken and sprinkle with the lime juice.

2 Heat 45ml/3 tbsp of the oil in a frying pan or griddle and cook the chicken escalopes for 10–12 minutes on each side, turning frequently.

3 Meanwhile, put the new potatoes and carrots in a small pan with the remaining oil and season with sea salt. Cover and cook over a medium heat for 10–15 minutes, stirring frequently.

4 Add the fennel and cook for a further 5 minutes, stirring frequently. Finally, add the asparagus and peas and cook for 5 minutes more, or until all the vegetables are tender and cooked.

5 To make the tomato mayonnaise, mix together the mayonnaise and sun-dried tomato purée in a small bowl. Spoon the vegetables on to a warmed serving platter or individual plates and arrange the chicken on top. Serve the tomato mayonnaise with the chicken and vegetables. Garnish with sprigs of flat leaf parsley.

COOK'S TIP
Any combinations of baby vegetables can be used. The weight specified is for prepared vegetables. Adjust the cooking time or the order in which they are added to the pan according to how long the chosen vegetables take to cook, for example add root vegetables first, before quick-cooking ones such as courgettes (zucchini), mangetouts (snow peas) or green beans.

ROAST LEG of LAMB

Tender young organic lamb is available only in the springtime, and is often served with a sauce using the first sprigs of mint of the year and early new potatoes. If you buy organic young lamb you can be happy in the knowledge that countryside seasons are being utilized and respected, and that the meat is fresh.

SERVES SIX

1.5kg/3¼lb leg of lamb
4 garlic cloves, sliced
2 fresh rosemary sprigs
30ml/2 tbsp light olive oil
300ml/½ pint/1¼ cups red wine
5ml/1 tsp honey
45ml/3 tbsp redcurrant jelly
sea salt and ground black pepper
spring vegetables, to serve

For the roast potatoes
45ml/3 tbsp olive oil
1.3kg/3lb potatoes, such as Desirée,
    peeled and cut into chunks

For the mint sauce
about 15g/½oz fresh mint
10ml/2 tsp unrefined caster (superfine)
    sugar or rapadura
15ml/1 tbsp boiling water
30ml/2 tbsp white wine vinegar

1 Preheat the oven to 220°C/425°F/ Gas 7. Make small slits into the lamb all over the joint. Press a slice of garlic and a few rosemary leaves into each slit, then place the joint in a roasting pan and season well. Drizzle the oil over the lamb and roast for about 1 hour.

COOK'S TIP
To make a quick and tasty gravy from the pan juices, add about 300ml/½ pint/ 1¼ cups red wine, stock or water and boil, stirring occasionally, until reduced and well flavoured. Season to taste, then strain into a sauce boat to serve.

2 Meanwhile, mix the wine, honey and redcurrant jelly in a small pan and heat, stirring, until the jelly melts. Bring to the boil, then reduce the heat and simmer until reduced by half. Spoon this glaze over the lamb and return it to the oven for 30–45 minutes.

3 To make the potatoes, put the oil in a roasting pan on the shelf above the meat. Boil the potatoes for 5–10 minutes, then drain them and fluff up the surface of each with a fork.

4 Add the prepared potatoes to the hot oil and baste well, then roast them for 45 minutes, or until they are crisp.

5 While the potatoes are roasting, make the mint sauce. Place the mint on a chopping board and scatter the sugar over the top. Chop the mint finely, then transfer to a bowl.

6 Add the boiling water and stir until the sugar has dissolved. Add 15ml/1 tbsp vinegar and taste the sauce before adding the remaining vinegar. (You may want to add slightly less or more than the suggested quantity.) Leave the mint sauce to stand until you are ready to serve the meal.

7 Remove the lamb from the oven, cover it loosely with foil and set it aside in a warm place to rest for 10–15 minutes before carving. Serve with the crisp roast potatoes, mint sauce and a selection of seasonal spring vegetables.

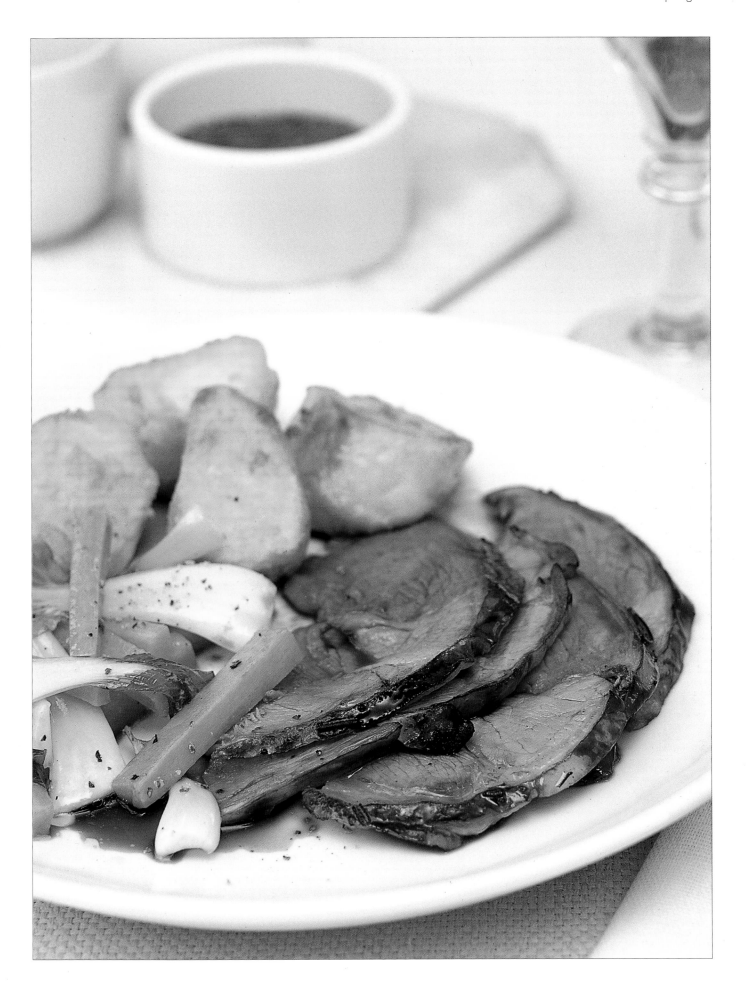

HERB-CRUSTED RACK of LAMB with PUY LENTILS

This lamb roast is quick and easy to prepare but looks impressive when served – it is the perfect choice when entertaining. Puy lentils are a favourite ingredient in the south of France. Their delicate flavour is the perfect complement to the rich meat.

SERVES FOUR

2 × 6-bone racks of lamb, chined
50g/2oz/1 cup fresh white or wholemeal
    (whole-wheat) breadcrumbs
2 large garlic cloves, crushed
90ml/6 tbsp chopped mixed fresh herbs,
    plus extra sprigs to garnish
50g/2oz/¼ cup butter, melted or
    50ml/3½ tbsp olive oil
sea salt and ground black pepper
new potatoes, to serve

For the Puy lentils
1 red onion, chopped
30ml/2 tbsp olive oil
400g/14oz can Puy lentils, rinsed
    and drained
400g/14oz can chopped tomatoes
30ml/2 tbsp chopped fresh flat leaf parsley

1 Preheat the oven to 220°C/425°F/ Gas 7. Trim any excess fat from the lamb, and season with salt and pepper.

2 Mix together the breadcrumbs, garlic, herbs and butter or oil, and press on to the fat-sides of the lamb. Place in a roasting pan and roast for 25 minutes. Cover with foil; stand for 5 minutes before carving.

3 Cook the onion in the olive oil until softened. Add the lentils and tomatoes and cook gently for 5 minutes, or until the lentils are piping hot. Stir in the parsley and season to taste.

4 Cut each rack of lamb in half and serve with the lentils and new potatoes. Garnish with herb sprigs.

LAMB BURGERS with RED ONION and TOMATO RELISH

A sharp-sweet red onion relish works well with burgers based on Middle Eastern style lamb. Serve with pitta bread and tabbouleh for an authentic taste, though baked potatoes and a crisp green salad are also good.

SERVES FOUR

25g/1oz/3 tbsp bulgur wheat
500g/1¼lb lean minced (ground) lamb
1 small red onion, finely chopped
2 garlic cloves, finely chopped
1 green chilli, seeded and finely chopped
5ml/1 tsp ground toasted cumin seeds
2.5ml/½ tsp ground sumac (optional)
15g/½oz/¼ cup chopped fresh flat
   leaf parsley
30ml/2 tbsp chopped fresh mint
olive oil, for frying
sea salt and ground black pepper

For the relish
2 red (bell) peppers, halved and seeded
2 red onions, cut into 5mm/¼in thick slices
75–90ml/5–6 tbsp extra virgin olive oil
350g/12oz cherry tomatoes, chopped
½–1 fresh red or green chilli, seeded
   and finely chopped (optional)
30ml/2 tbsp chopped fresh mint
30ml/2 tbsp chopped fresh parsley
15ml/1 tbsp chopped fresh oregano
   or marjoram
2.5–5ml/½–1 tsp each ground toasted
   cumin seeds
2.5–5ml/½–1 tsp sumac (optional)
juice of ½ lemon
unrefined caster (superfine) sugar
   or rapadura, to taste

1 Pour 150ml/¼ pint/⅔ cup hot water over the bulgur wheat in a mixing bowl and leave to stand for 15 minutes, then drain the wheat in a sieve and squeeze out the excess moisture.

2 To make the relish, grill (broil) the peppers, skin side up, until the skin chars and blisters. Place in a bowl, cover and leave to stand for 10 minutes. Peel off the skin, dice the peppers finely and place in a bowl.

3 Brush the onions with 15ml/1 tbsp oil and grill for 5 minutes on each side, until browned. Leave to cool.

4 Place the bulgur in a bowl and add the minced lamb, onion, garlic, chilli, cumin, sumac, if using, parsley and mint. Mix the ingredients thoroughly together by hand, then season with 2.5ml/½ tsp salt and plenty of black pepper and mix again. Form the mixture into eight small burgers.

5 Chop the onions for the relish. Add with the tomatoes, chilli to taste, herbs and 2.5ml/½ tsp each of the cumin and sumac, if using, to the peppers. Stir in 60ml/4 tbsp of the remaining oil and 15ml/1 tbsp of the lemon juice. Season with salt, pepper and sugar and leave to stand for 20–30 minutes.

6 Heat a heavy frying pan over a high heat and grease lightly with olive oil. Cook the burgers for about 5–6 minutes on each side, or until just cooked at the centre.

7 While the burgers are cooking, taste the relish and adjust the seasoning, adding more pepper, sugar, oil, chilli, cumin, sumac, if using, and lemon juice to taste. Serve the burgers with the relish.

SALMON FISH CAKES

The secret of a good fish cake is to make it with freshly prepared fish and potatoes, home-made breadcrumbs and plenty of fresh herbs, such as dill and parsley or tarragon. Serve simply with rocket leaves and lemon wedges.

SERVES FOUR

450g/1lb cooked salmon fillet
450g/1lb freshly cooked potatoes, mashed
25g/1oz/2 tbsp butter, melted or
　　30ml/2 tbsp olive oil
10ml/2 tsp wholegrain mustard
15ml/1 tbsp each chopped fresh dill and
　　chopped fresh parsley or tarragon
grated rind and juice of ½ lemon
15g/½oz/2 tbsp wholemeal
　　(whole-wheat) flour
1 egg, lightly beaten
150g/5oz/2 cups dried breadcrumbs
60ml/4 tbsp sunflower oil
sea salt and ground black pepper
rocket (arugula) leaves and chives, to garnish
lemon wedges, to serve

1 Flake the cooked salmon, discarding any skin and bones. Put it in a bowl with the mashed potato, melted butter or oil and wholegrain mustard, and mix well. Stir in the herbs and the lemon rind and juice. Season to taste with plenty of sea salt and ground black pepper.

2 Divide the mixture into eight portions and shape each into a ball, then flatten into a thick disc. Dip the fish cakes first in flour, then in egg and finally in breadcrumbs, making sure that they are evenly coated with crumbs.

3 Heat the oil in a frying pan until it is very hot. Fry the fish cakes in batches until golden brown and crisp all over. As each batch is ready, drain on kitchen paper and keep hot. Garnish with rocket and chives and serve with lemon wedges.

COOK'S TIP

Any fresh white or hot-smoked fish is suitable. Always buy organically farmed fish, or sustainably caught wild fish.

FILLETS of SEA BREAM in FILO PASTRY

Any firm fish fillets can be used for this dish — bass, grouper and red mullet or snapper are particularly good — and, as the number of organic seawater fish farms grows, an increasing variety of breeds is becoming available. Each parcel is a meal in itself and can be prepared several hours in advance.

3 Thinly slice the potatoes lengthways. Brush a baking sheet with a little of the oil. Lay a sheet of filo pastry on the sheet, brush it with oil, then lay a second sheet crossways over the first. Repeat with two more pastry sheets. Arrange a quarter of the sliced potatoes in the centre, season and add a quarter of the shredded sorrel. Lay a bream fillet on top, skin-side up. Season.

4 Loosely fold the filo pastry up and over to make a neat parcel. Make three more parcels; place on the baking sheet. Brush with half the melted butter or oil. Bake for about 20 minutes until the filo is puffed up and golden brown.

5 Meanwhile, make the sorrel sauce. Heat the remaining butter or oil in a pan, add the reserved sorrel and cook gently for 3 minutes, stirring, until it wilts. Stir in the stock and cream. Heat almost to boiling point, stirring so that the sorrel breaks down. Season to taste and keep hot until the fish parcels are ready. Serve garnished with red pepper and salad leaves. Hand round the sauce separately.

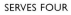

SERVES FOUR

8 small waxy salad potatoes, preferably red-skinned
200g/7oz sorrel, stalks removed
30ml/2 tbsp olive oil
16 filo pastry sheets, thawed if frozen
4 sea bream fillets, about 175g/6oz each, scaled but not skinned
50g/2oz/¼ cup butter, melted or 60ml/4 tbsp olive oil
120ml/4fl oz/½ cup fish stock
250ml/8fl oz/1 cup whipping cream or soya cream
sea salt and ground black pepper
finely diced red (bell) pepper and salad leaves, to garnish

VARIATION
Use small spinach leaves or baby chard in place of the sorrel.

1 Preheat the oven to 200°C/400°F/ Gas 6. Cook the potatoes in a pan of lightly salted boiling water for about 20 minutes, or until just tender. Drain and leave to cool.

2 Set about half the sorrel leaves aside. Shred the remaining leaves by piling up six or eight at a time, rolling them up like a fat cigar and slicing them.

FROZEN CLEMENTINES

*These pretty, sorbet-filled fruits store well in the freezer, so make them well in advance
and they will be perfect for an impromptu dinner party. Organic citrus fruit has a matt
skin — evidence that they have not been coated with shiny anti-fungal wax.*

MAKES TWELVE

16 large clementines or small oranges
175g/6oz/scant 1 cup unrefined caster
    (superfine) sugar or rapadura
105ml/7 tbsp water
juice of 2 lemons
a little fresh orange juice (if necessary)
fresh mint leaves, to decorate

1 Carefully slice the tops off 12 of the clementines to make lids. Place the lids on a baking sheet. Loosen the clementine flesh with a sharp knife then carefully scoop it out into a mixing bowl, keeping the shells intact. Scrape out as much of the membrane from the shells as possible. Place the shells on the baking tray and place the tray in the freezer.

2 Put the sugar and water in a heavy pan and heat gently, stirring until the unrefined caster sugar or rapadura dissolves. Boil for 3 minutes without stirring, then leave the syrup to cool. Stir in the lemon juice.

3 Grate the rind from the remaining four clementines. Squeeze the fruits and add the juice and rind to the lemon syrup.

4 Process the clementine flesh in a food processor or blender, then press it through a sieve placed over a bowl to extract as much juice as possible. Add this to the syrup. You need about 900ml/ 1½ pints/3¾ cups of liquid. Make up to the required amount with fresh orange juice if necessary.

5 If making by hand, pour the mixture into a shallow plastic container and freeze for 3–4 hours, beating twice as the sorbet thickens to break up the ice crystals. If using an ice cream maker, churn the mixture until it holds its shape.

6 Gently pack the citrus sorbet into the clementine shells, mounding them up slightly in the centre. Position the lids on top and return the fruit to the freezer for several hours, or until the sorbet is frozen solid.

7 Transfer the frozen clementines to the refrigerator about 30 minutes before serving, to allow the sorbet to soften a little. Serve on individual plates and decorate with fresh mint leaves.

RHUBARB and GINGER ICE CREAM

The tangy combination of gently poached rhubarb and chopped ginger is blended with mascarpone to create this pretty blush-pink ice cream. Look for tender slim stalks of forced rhubarb in spring – it has a delicate pink colour and a delicious flavour.

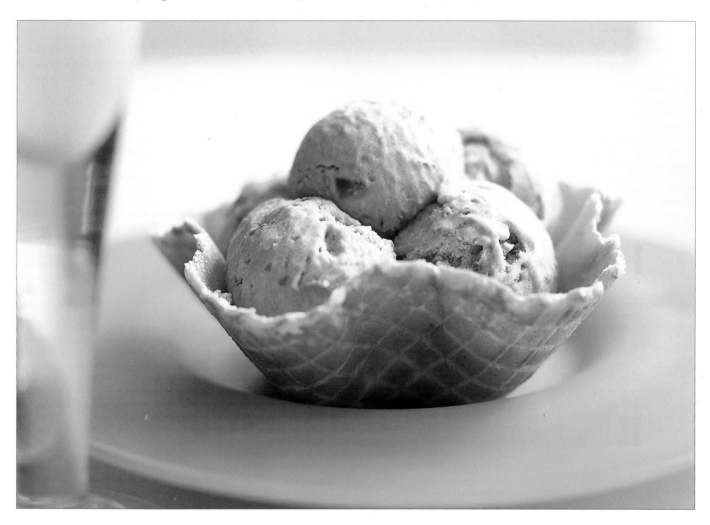

SERVES FOUR TO SIX

5 pieces of preserved stem ginger
450g/1lb trimmed rhubarb, sliced
115g/4oz/generous ½ cup unrefined
   caster (superfine) sugar or rapadura
30ml/2 tbsp water
150g/5oz/⅔ cup mascarpone cheese
150ml/¼ pint/⅔ cup whipping cream
   or soya cream
wafer baskets, to serve (optional)

1 Using a sharp knife, roughly chop the preserved stem ginger and set it aside. Put the rhubarb slices into a pan and add the sugar and water. Bring to the boil, then cover and simmer for about 5 minutes until the rhubarb is just tender and still bright pink.

2 Tip the mixture into a food processor or blender, process until smooth, then leave to cool. Chill if time permits.

3 If making by hand, in a bowl, mix together the mascarpone, cream and stem ginger with the rhubarb purée. Pour the mixture into a plastic tub and freeze for 6 hours, or until firm, beating the mixture once or twice during the freezing time to break up the ice crystals.

COOK'S TIP

Rapadura is an alternative to refined sugar. It is made by sun-drying organic sugar cane juice and has a similar colour and texture to soft brown sugar, but has more flavour and is more nutritious.

4 If using an ice cream maker, churn the purée for 15–20 minutes until it is thick. Put the mascarpone into a bowl, soften it with a wooden spoon, then beat in the cream. Add the stem ginger, then churn in the ice cream maker until firm. Serve scoops of the ice cream in bowls or wafer baskets.

RHUBARB MERINGUE PIE

The sharp tang of tender forced rhubarb with its sweet meringue topping will really tantalize the taste buds. This pudding is delicious hot or cold with cream or vanilla ice cream.

SERVES SIX

200g/7oz/1¾ cups plain (all-purpose) flour, plus extra for flouring
25g/1oz/¼ cup ground walnuts
115g/4oz/½ cup chilled butter or non-hydrogenated magarine, diced
275g/10oz/generous 1½ cups unrefined caster (superfine) sugar or rapadura
4 egg yolks
675g/1½lb rhubarb, cut into small pieces
grated rind and juice of 3 oranges
75ml/5 tbsp cornflour (cornstarch)
3 egg whites
whipped cream or soya cream, to serve

1 Sift the flour into a bowl and add the ground walnuts. Rub in the butter until the mixture resembles fine breadcrumbs. Stir in 30ml/2 tbsp of the sugar with 1 egg yolk beaten with 15ml/1 tbsp water. Mix to a firm dough. Turn out on to a floured surface and knead. Wrap in a plastic bag and chill for 30 minutes.

2 Preheat the oven to 190°C/375°F/ Gas 5. Roll out the pastry on a floured surface and use to line a 23cm/9in fluted flan tin (quiche pan). Prick the base with a fork. Line with foil and fill with baking beans. Bake for 15 minutes.

3 Put the rhubarb, 75g/3oz/6 tbsp of the remaining sugar and the orange rind in a pan. Cover and cook gently until the rhubarb is tender.

4 Remove the foil and beans from the pastry case, then brush with a little of the remaining egg yolk. Bake for 10–15 minutes until the pastry is crisp.

5 Blend together the cornflour and the orange juice in a small bowl. Remove from the heat, stir the cornflour mixture into the cooked rhubarb, then bring back to the boil, stirring constantly until thickened. Cook for a further 1–2 minutes. Allow the mixture to cool slightly, then beat in the remaining egg yolks. Pour into the cooked pastry case, spreading it evenly.

6 Whisk the egg whites in a large mixing bowl until they form soft peaks, then gradually whisk in the remaining sugar, 15ml/1 tbsp at a time, whisking well after each addition.

7 Spoon the meringue over the filling to cover completely. Bake for 25 minutes until golden. Serve warm, or leave to cool for about 30 minutes and serve with whipped cream.

TUSCAN CITRUS SPONGE

This tangy cake comes from the little Tuscan town of Pitigliano. It is a light and airy whisked sponge made with matzo and potato flours rather than traditional wheat flour.

SERVES SIX TO EIGHT

12 eggs, separated
300g/11oz/1½ cups unrefined caster
   (superfine) sugar or rapadura
120ml/4fl oz/½ cup fresh orange juice
grated rind of 1 orange
grated rind of 1 lemon
50g/2oz/½ cup potato flour, sifted
90g/3½oz/¾ cup fine matzo meal or
   matzo meal flour, sifted
unrefined icing (confectioner's) sugar,
   for dusting
orange juice and segments of orange,
   to serve

1 Preheat the oven to 160°C/325°F/ Gas 3. Whisk the egg yolks until pale and frothy, then whisk in the sugar, orange juice, orange rind and lemon rind.

2 Fold the sifted flours or flour and meal into the egg and sugar mixture. In a clean bowl, whisk the egg whites until stiff, then fold into the egg yolk mixture.

VARIATION
Omit the lemon and replace the orange with two blood oranges for a really fresh fruity flavour.

3 Pour the cake mixture into a deep, ungreased 25cm/10in cake tin (pan) and bake for about 1 hour, or until a cocktail stick (toothpick), inserted in the centre, comes out clean. Leave to cool in the tin.

4 When cold, turn out the cake and invert on to a serving plate. Dust with a little icing sugar and serve in wedges with orange segments, moistened with a little fresh orange juice.

COOK'S TIPS
• When testing to see if the cake is cooked, if you don't have a cocktail stick to hand, use a strand of raw dried spaghetti instead – it will work just as well.
• If you cannot find organic matzo meal, try fine polenta instead.

SUMMER

The abundance of fresh produce at this time of year makes summer a wonderful time for any cook. With hot, sunny days and long, balmy evenings for picnics and barbecues, summer eating is a sheer delight. Chilled dishes are easy to prepare in advance: choose the classic Vichyssoise or the popular Japanese Cold Somen Noodles. Or take your pick from the wide selection of colourful salads, including Tabbouleh and Country Pasta Salad, to make the most of the dazzling array of organic fruit and vegetables available now. If you fancy cooking outside, try barbecueing Marinated Beef with Onion Rings, and accompany them with organic bread and a green salad for a simple meal. With a wide selection of mouthwatering juicy fruits in season, summer desserts really are special. Try a refreshing Watermelon Granita or, if you want something really indulgent, Coffee Crêpes with Peaches and Cream, or Blueberry Frangipane Flan. Summer is also the beginning of the preserving season and you just can't beat home-made strawberry jam served with freshly baked scones and cream – delicious!

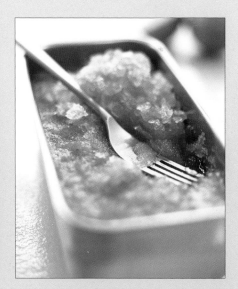

VICHYSSOISE

This classic, chilled summer soup is based on the flavourful combination of leeks and potatoes, made luxuriously velvety by adding dairy or soya cream.

SERVES FOUR TO SIX

50g/2oz/¼ cup unsalted (sweet) butter or
   50ml/3½ tbsp olive oil
450g/1lb leeks, white parts only, sliced
3 large shallots, sliced
250g/9oz floury potatoes (such as
   Maris Piper), peeled and cut
   into chunks
1 litre/1¾ pints/4 cups light chicken stock
   or water
300ml/½ pint/1¼ cups double (heavy)
   cream or soya cream
a little lemon juice (optional)
sea salt and ground black pepper
fresh chives, to garnish

1 Heat the butter or oil in a heavy pan. Add the leeks and shallots and cook gently, covered, for 15–20 minutes, stirring once or twice, until soft but not browned.

2 Add the potato chunks to the pan and cook, uncovered, for a few minutes, stirring occasionally.

3 Stir in the light chicken stock or water, 5ml/1 tsp sea salt and ground pepper to taste. Bring to the boil, then reduce the heat and partly cover the pan. Simmer for 15 minutes, or until the potatoes are soft.

4 Cool, then process the soup until smooth in a food processor or blender. Pour the soup into a bowl and stir in the cream. Season to taste.

5 Chill the soup for at least 4 hours or until very cold. Taste the chilled soup for seasoning and add a squeeze of lemon juice, if required. Pour the soup into bowls and garnish with chives.

COLD SOMEN NOODLES

At the height of summer, cold somen noodles served immersed in ice cold water and accompanied by sauces and relishes make a refreshing and exotic meal.

SERVES FOUR

300g/11oz dried somen or soba noodles

For the dipping sauce
105ml/7 tbsp mirin
2.5ml/½ tsp sea salt
105ml/7 tbsp shoyu
20g/¾oz kezuri-bushi
400ml/14fl oz/1⅔ cups water

For the relishes
2 spring onions (scallions), trimmed and
    finely chopped
2.5cm/1in fresh root ginger, peeled and
    finely grated
2 shiso or basil leaves, finely
    chopped (optional)
30ml/2 tbsp toasted sesame seeds

For the garnishes
10cm/4in cucumber
5ml/1 tsp sea salt
ice cubes or a block of ice
ice-cold water
115g/4oz cooked, peeled small
    prawns (shrimp)
orchid flowers or nasturtium flowers
    and leaves (optional)

1 To make the dipping sauce, put the mirin in a pan and bring to the boil to evaporate the alcohol. Add the salt and shoyu and shake the pan gently to mix. Add the kezuri-bushi and mix with the liquid. Add the water to the pan and bring to the boil. Cook over a vigorous heat for 3 minutes without stirring. Remove from the heat and strain through a muslin bag. Leave to cool, then chill for at least an hour.

2 Prepare the cucumber garnish. If the cucumber is bigger than 4cm/1½in in diameter, cut in half and scoop out the seeds, then slice thinly. For a smaller cucumber, first cut into 5cm/2in lengths, then use a vegetable peeler to remove the seeds and make a hole in the centre. Slice thinly. Sprinkle with the salt and leave in a sieve for 20 minutes, then rinse in cold water and drain.

3 Bring at least 1.5 litres/2½ pints/6¼ cups water to the boil in a large pan. Meanwhile, untie the bundle of somen. Have 75ml/2½fl oz/⅓ cup cold water to hand. Somen only take 2 minutes to cook. Put the somen in the rapidly boiling water. When it foams again, pour the glass of water in. When the water boils again, the somen are ready. Drain into a colander. Rinse under cold running water, and rub the somen with your hands to remove the starch. Drain well.

4 Put some ice cubes or a block of ice in the centre of a chilled, large glass bowl, and add the somen. Gently pour on enough ice-cold water to cover the somen, then arrange cucumber slices, prawns and flowers, if using, on top.

5 Prepare all the relishes separately in small dishes or small sake cups.

6 Divide approximately one-third of the dipping sauce among four small cups. Put the remaining sauce in a jug (pitcher) or gravy boat.

7 Serve the noodles cold with the relishes. The guests are invited to put any combination of relishes into their dipping-sauce cup. Hold the cup over the somen bowl, pick up a mouthful of somen, then dip them into the sauce and eat. Add more dipping sauce from the jug and more relishes as required.

TABBOULEH

This is a wonderfully refreshing, tangy salad of soaked bulgur wheat and masses of fresh organic mint and parsley. Increase the amount of fresh herbs for a greener salad.

SERVES FOUR TO SIX

250g/9oz/1½ cups bulgur wheat
1 large bunch spring onions (scallions),
   thinly sliced
1 cucumber, finely chopped or diced
3 tomatoes, chopped
1.5–2.5ml/¼–½ tsp ground cumin
1 large bunch fresh flat leaf
   parsley, chopped
1 large bunch fresh mint, chopped
juice of 2 lemons, or to taste
60ml/4 tbsp extra virgin olive oil
cos or romaine lettuce leaves
olives, lemon wedges, tomato wedges,
   cucumber slices and mint sprigs,
   to garnish (optional)
natural (plain) yogurt, to serve (optional)

1 Pick over the bulgur wheat to remove any dirt. Place it in a bowl, cover with cold water and leave to soak for about 30 minutes. Tip the bulgur wheat into a sieve and drain well, shaking to remove any excess water, then return it to the bowl.

2 Add the spring onions to the bulgur wheat, then mix and squeeze together with your hands to combine.

3 Add the cucumber, tomatoes, cumin, parsley, mint, lemon juice and oil to the bulgur wheat and toss well.

4 Heap the tabbouleh on to a bed of lettuce leaves and garnish with olives, lemon wedges, tomato, cucumber and mint sprigs, if you like. Serve with a bowl of natural yogurt, if you like.

VARIATION
Use couscous soaked in boiling water in place of the bulgur wheat and use fresh coriander (cilantro) instead of parsley.

TOMATO and MOZZARELLA SALAD

Sweet naturally ripened organic tomatoes and fresh basil capture the essence of summer in this simple salad. Choose plum or beefsteak tomatoes for this dish.

SERVES FOUR

5 ripe tomatoes
2 × 225g/8oz buffalo mozzarella cheeses,
   drained and sliced
I small red onion, chopped

For the dressing
½ small garlic clove, peeled
15g/½oz/½ cup fresh basil leaves
30ml/2 tbsp chopped fresh flat
   leaf parsley
25ml/1½ tbsp small salted capers, rinsed
2.5ml/½ tsp mustard
75–90ml/5–6 tbsp extra virgin olive oil
5–10ml/1–2 tsp balsamic vinegar
ground black pepper

For the garnish
fresh basil leaves
fresh parsley sprigs

I First make the dressing. Put the garlic, basil, parsley, half the capers and the mustard in a food processor or blender and process briefly to chop. Then, with the motor running, gradually pour in the olive oil through the feeder tube to make a smooth purée with a dressing consistency. Add the balsamic vinegar to taste and season with plenty of ground black pepper.

2 Slice the tomatoes. Arrange the tomato and mozzarella slices on a plate. Scatter the onion over and season with a little ground black pepper.

3 Drizzle the dressing over the salad, then scatter a few basil leaves, parsley sprigs and the remaining capers on top as a garnish. Leave for 10–15 minutes before serving.

SUMMER SALAD

*Ripe organic tomatoes, mozzarella and olives make a good base for a fresh and tangy
pasta salad that is perfect for a light summer lunch.*

SERVES FOUR

350g/12oz/3 cups dried penne
150g/5oz packet buffalo mozzarella,
    drained and diced
3 ripe tomatoes, diced
10 pitted black olives, sliced
10 pitted green olives, sliced
1 spring onion (scallion), thinly sliced on
    the diagonal
1 handful fresh basil leaves

For the dressing
90ml/6 tbsp extra virgin olive oil
15ml/1 tbsp balsamic vinegar or
    lemon juice
sea salt and ground black pepper

COOK'S TIP
Mozzarella made from buffalo milk
has more flavour than the type made
with cow's milk. Look for *mozzarella de
buffalo* in your organic store.

1 Cook the pasta for 10–12 minutes,
or according to the instructions on the
packet. Tip it into a colander and rinse
briefly under cold running water, then
shake the colander to remove as much
water as possible and leave to drain.

VARIATION
Make the salad more substantial by adding
sliced peppers, flaked tuna, anchovy fillets
or diced ham. Always choose sustainably
caught tuna and anchovies.

2 Make the dressing. Whisk the olive oil
and balsamic vinegar or lemon juice in a
jug (pitcher) with a little salt and pepper
to taste.

3 Place the pasta, mozzarella, tomatoes,
olives and spring onion in a large bowl,
pour the dressing over and toss together
well. Taste for seasoning before serving,
sprinkled with basil leaves.

COUNTRY PASTA SALAD

*Colourful, tasty and nutritious, this is the ideal pasta salad for a summer picnic. A variety
of organic pasta is available – any medium-size shapes are suitable for this salad.*

SERVES SIX

300g/11oz/2¾ cups dried fusilli
150g/5oz fine green beans,
    trimmed and cut into
    5cm/2in lengths
1 potato, about 150g/5oz, diced
200g/7oz cherry tomatoes, halved
2 spring onions (scallions),
    finely chopped
90g/3½oz/scant 1¼ cups Parmesan
    cheese or premium Italian-style
    vegetarian cheese, coarsely shaved
6–8 pitted black olives, cut into rings
15–30ml/1–2 tbsp capers, to taste

For the dressing
90ml/6 tbsp extra virgin olive oil
15ml/1 tbsp balsamic vinegar
15ml/1 tbsp chopped fresh flat leaf parsley
sea salt and ground black pepper

1 Cook the pasta according to the
instructions on the packet. Drain it into
a colander, rinse under cold running
water until cold, then shake the colander
to remove as much water as possible.
Leave to drain and dry.

2 Cook the beans and diced potato in a
pan of boiling water for 5–6 minutes or
steam for 8–10 minutes. Drain and let cool.

3 To make the dressing, put all the
ingredients in a large bowl with a little
sea salt and ground black pepper to
taste and whisk well to mix.

4 Add the tomatoes, spring onions,
Parmesan, olive rings and capers to the
dressing then stir in the cold pasta, beans
and potato. Toss well to mix. Cover and
leave to stand for about 30 minutes.
Taste for seasoning before serving.

VARIATIONS
Use other pasta shapes, such as penne or
conchiglie, instead of fusilli. Try wholemeal
pasta shapes for a nuttier taste. Other
summer vegetables – steamed courgettes
(zucchini) or mangetouts (snow peas), or
roasted red (bell) peppers – all taste
wonderful in this salad.

THAI BEEF SALAD

Meat does not need to dominate a meal, as this light Thai salad shows. Especially when cooking with good-quality organic meat, a little adds a lot of flavour.

SERVES FOUR

675g/1½lb fillet (tenderloin) or rump (round) beef steak
30ml/2 tbsp olive oil
2 small mild red chillies, seeded and sliced
225g/8oz/3¼ cups shiitake mushrooms, finely sliced

For the dressing
3 spring onions (scallions), finely chopped
2 garlic cloves, finely chopped
juice of 1 lime
15–30ml/1–2 tbsp fish or oyster sauce, to taste
5ml/1 tsp unrefined soft light brown sugar or rapadura
30ml/2 tbsp chopped fresh coriander (cilantro)

To serve
1 cos or romaine lettuce, torn into strips
175g/6oz cherry tomatoes, halved
5cm/2in piece cucumber, peeled, halved and thinly sliced
45ml/3 tbsp toasted sesame seeds

1 Preheat the grill (broiler) until hot, then cook the steak for 2–4 minutes on each side depending on how well done you like steak. (In Thailand, the beef is traditionally served quite rare.) Leave the beef to cool for at least 15 minutes.

2 Use a very sharp knife to slice the meat as thinly as possible and place the slices in a bowl.

VARIATION
If you can find them, yellow chillies make a colourful addition to this dish. Substitute one for one of the red chillies.

3 Heat the olive oil in a small frying pan. Add the seeded and sliced red chillies and the sliced mushrooms and cook for 5 minutes, stirring occasionally. Turn off the heat and add the grilled steak slices to the pan, then stir well to coat the beef slices in the cooked chilli and mushroom mixture.

4 Stir all the ingredients for the dressing together, then pour it over the meat mixture and toss gently.

5 Arrange the salad ingredients on a serving plate. Spoon the warm steak mixture in the centre and sprinkle the sesame seeds over. Serve at once.

FRESH TUNA SALAD NIÇOISE

This classic colourful salad is transformed into something really special by using fresh tuna. When buying tuna make sure it is line-caught tuna that is certified as sustainably caught by the Marine Stewardship Council (MSC).

SERVES FOUR

4 tuna steaks, about 150g/5oz each
30ml/2 tbsp olive oil
225g/8oz fine green beans, trimmed
1 small cos or romaine lettuce or
    2 Little Gem (Bibb) lettuces
4 new potatoes, boiled
4 ripe tomatoes, or 12 cherry tomatoes
2 red (bell) peppers, seeded and cut
    into thin strips
4 hard-boiled eggs, sliced
8 drained anchovy fillets in oil,
    halved lengthways (optional)
16 large black olives
sea salt and ground black pepper
12 fresh basil leaves, to garnish

For the dressing
15ml/1 tbsp red wine vinegar
90ml/6 tbsp olive oil
1 fat garlic clove, crushed

1 Brush the tuna on both sides with a little olive oil and season. Heat a ridged griddle or the grill (broiler) until very hot, then grill the tuna steaks for 1–2 minutes on each side; the flesh should be pink and juicy in the middle.

2 Cook the beans in a pan of lightly salted boiling water for 4–5 minutes, or until crisp-tender. Drain, refresh under cold water and drain again.

COOK'S TIP
To intensify the flavour of the peppers, grill (broil) them until the skins are charred, place in a bowl and cover with kitchen paper. Leave for 10–15 minutes, then rub off the skins.

3 Separate the lettuce leaves and rinse them thoroughly under cold running water and dry them on kitchen paper. Arrange them on four individual serving plates. Slice the cooked potatoes and tomatoes, if large (leave cherry tomatoes whole or halve them) and divide them among the plates. Arrange the beans and red pepper strips over the potatoes and tomatoes.

4 Shell the hard-boiled eggs and cut them into thick slices. Place a few slices of egg on each plate with the anchovy fillets, if using, and olives.

5 To make the dressing, whisk together the vinegar, olive oil and garlic and season to taste. Drizzle over the salads, arrange the tuna steaks on top, scatter over the basil and serve.

SPICED VEGETABLE COUSCOUS

This tasty vegetarian main course is easy to make and can be prepared with any number of seasonal organic vegetables such as spinach, peas, broad beans or corn.

SERVES SIX

45ml/3 tbsp olive oil
1 large onion, finely chopped
2 garlic cloves, crushed
15ml/1 tbsp tomato purée (paste)
2.5ml/½ tsp ground turmeric
2.5ml/½ tsp cayenne pepper
5ml/1 tsp ground coriander
5ml/1 tsp ground cumin
225g/8oz/1½ cups cauliflower florets
225g/8oz baby carrots, trimmed
1 red (bell) pepper, seeded and diced
225g/8oz courgettes (zucchini), sliced
400g/14oz can chickpeas, drained
  and rinsed
4 beefsteak tomatoes, skinned and sliced
45ml/3 tbsp chopped fresh coriander
  (cilantro)
sea salt and ground black pepper
coriander sprigs, to garnish

For the couscous
2.5ml/½ tsp sea salt
450g/1lb/2⅔ cups couscous
50g/2oz/¼ cup butter or
  50ml/3½ tbsp sunflower oil

1 Heat 30ml/2 tbsp oil in a large pan, add the onion and garlic and cook until soft and translucent. Stir in the tomato purée, turmeric, cayenne, coriander and cumin. Cook, stirring, for 2 minutes.

2 Add the cauliflower, baby carrots and pepper, with enough water to come halfway up the vegetables. Bring to the boil, then lower the heat, cover and simmer for 10 minutes.

3 Add the courgettes, chickpeas and tomatoes to the pan and cook for 10 minutes. Stir in the fresh coriander and season. Keep hot.

4 To cook the couscous, bring about 475ml/16fl oz/2 cups water to the boil in a large pan. Add the remaining olive oil and the salt. Remove from the heat and add the couscous, stirring. Allow to swell for 2 minutes.

5 Add the butter or sunflower oil, and heat through gently, stirring to separate the grains.

6 Turn the couscous out on to a warm serving dish, and spoon the cooked vegetables on top, pouring over any liquid. Garnish with coriander and serve immediately.

MARINATED BEEF with ONION RINGS

Mexican chillies combine well with garlic in this marinade for grilled steak. Organic beef is tastier and has a better balance of cholesterol than the non-organic kind.

SERVES FOUR

20g/¾oz large mild dried red chillies
    (such as mulato or pasilla)
2 garlic cloves, plain or smoked,
    finely chopped
5ml/1 tsp ground toasted cumin seeds
5ml/1 tsp dried oregano
60ml/4 tbsp olive oil
4 × 175–225g/6–8oz beef steaks, rump
    (round) or rib-eye
sea salt and ground black pepper

For the onion rings
2 onions, sliced into rings
250ml/8fl oz/1 cup milk or soya milk
75g/3oz/¾ cup coarse corn meal
2.5ml/½ tsp dried red chilli flakes
5ml/1 tsp ground toasted cumin seeds
5ml/1 tsp dried oregano
sunflower or safflower oil,
    for deep-frying

1 Cut the stalks from the dried red chillies and discard the seeds. Toast the chillies in a dry frying pan over a high heat, stirring constantly, for 2–4 minutes, until they give off their aroma. Place the chillies in a bowl, cover with warm water and leave them to soak for 20–30 minutes. Drain the chillies and reserve the soaking water.

2 Process the soaked, drained chillies to a paste with the finely chopped garlic, toasted cumin seeds, oregano and oil in a food processor. Add a little of the soaking water, if needed. Season with ground black pepper.

3 Wash and dry the steaks, place them in a non-metallic container, rub the chilli paste all over them and leave to marinate in the refrigerator for up to 12 hours.

4 To make the onion rings, soak the onion slices in the milk for 30 minutes. Mix the corn meal, chilli, cumin and oregano, and season with salt and pepper.

5 Heat the oil for deep-frying in a deep pan to 160–180°C/325–350°F, or until a cube of day-old bread turns brown in about a minute.

6 Drain the onion rings and dip each one into the corn meal mixture, coating it thoroughly. Fry for 2–4 minutes until browned and crisp. Do not overcrowd the pan, but cook in batches. Lift the onion rings out of the pan with a slotted spoon and drain on kitchen paper.

7 Heat a barbecue or cast-iron griddle. Season the steaks with salt and cook for about 4 minutes on each side for a medium result; reduce or increase this time according to how rare or well done you like steak. Serve the steaks with the onion rings.

WATERMELON GRANITA

Pastel pink flakes of ice, subtly blended with the citrus freshness of lime and the delicate, refreshing flavour of organic watermelon, make this granita a treat for the eye and the tastebuds.

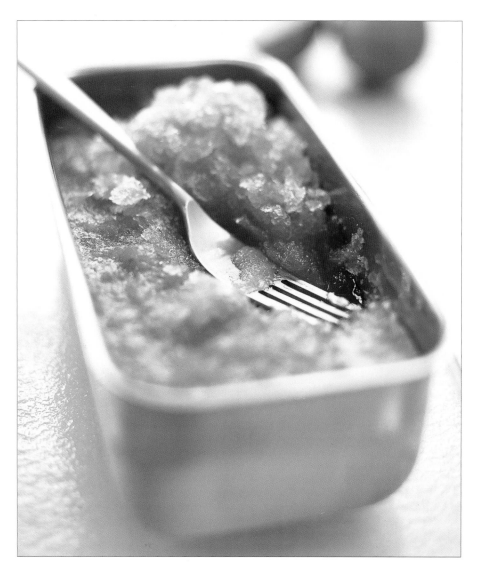

2 Bring the sugar and water to the boil in a small pan, stirring constantly until the sugar has dissolved. Pour the syrup into a bowl. Allow the syrup to cool, then chill until needed.

3 Strain the purée through a sieve into a large plastic container. Discard the melon seeds. Pour in the chilled syrup, lime rind and juice and mix well.

4 Cover and freeze for 2 hours until the granita mixture around the sides of the container is mushy. Mash the ice finely with a fork and return to the freezer.

5 Freeze for a further 2 hours, mashing the mixture every 30 minutes, until the granita has a slushy consistency. Scoop it into individual dishes and serve with the wedges of lime.

SERVES SIX

1 whole watermelon,
    about 1.8–2kg/4–4½lb
150g/5oz/¾ cup unrefined caster
    (superfine) sugar or rapadura
150ml/¼ pint/⅔ cup water
finely grated rind and juice
    of 2 limes
lime wedges, to decorate

COOK'S TIP
If you are using another melon, such as cantaloupe or Charentais, you may not need as much lime juice. Add half in step 3, then taste the mixture and adjust as necessary.

1 Cut the watermelon into quarters. Discard most of the seeds, scoop the flesh into a food processor and process briefly until smooth. Alternatively, use a blender, and process the watermelon quarters in small batches.

VARIATION
To serve this granita cocktail-style, dip the rim of each glass serving dish in a little water, then dip it into unrefined caster (superfine) sugar. Spoon in the granita, pour over a little Tequila and decorate with lime wedges.

FROZEN MELON

Freezing sorbet in hollowed out fruit, which is then cut into icy wedges, is an excellent idea. The refreshing flavour makes this dessert irresistible on a hot summer's day.

SERVES SIX

50g/2oz/¼ cup unrefined caster (superfine) sugar or rapadura
30ml/2 tbsp clear honey
15ml/1 tbsp lemon juice
60ml/4 tbsp water
1 medium cantaloupe melon or Charentais melon, about 1 kg/2¼lb
crushed ice, cucumber slices and borage flowers, to decorate

1 Put the sugar, honey, lemon juice and water in a heavy pan, and heat gently until the sugar dissolves. Bring to the boil, and boil for 1 minute, without stirring, to make a syrup. Leave to cool.

2 Cut the cantaloupe or Charentais melon in half and discard the seeds. Carefully scoop out the flesh using a metal spoon or melon baller and place in a food processor, taking care to keep the halved shells intact.

3 Blend the melon flesh until very smooth, then transfer to a mixing bowl. Stir in the cooled sugar syrup and chill until very cold. Invert the melon shells and leave them to drain on kitchen paper for a few minutes, then transfer them to the freezer while making the sorbet.

4 If making by hand, pour the mixture into a container and freeze for 3–4 hours, beating well twice with a fork, a whisk or in a food processor, to break up the ice crystals and produce a smooth texture. If using an ice cream maker, churn the melon mixture in the ice cream maker until the sorbet holds its shape.

5 Pack the sorbet into the melon shells and level the surface with a knife. Use a dessertspoon to scoop out the centre of each filled melon shell to simulate the seed cavity. Freeze the prepared fruit overnight until firm.

6 To serve, use a large knife to cut each melon half into three wedges. Serve on a bed of ice on a large platter or individual serving plates, and decorate with the cucumber slices and borage flowers.

COOK'S TIP
If the melon sorbet is too firm to cut when taken straight from the freezer, let it soften in the refrigerator for 10–20 minutes. Take care when slicing the frozen melon shell into wedges. A serrated kitchen knife is easier to work with.

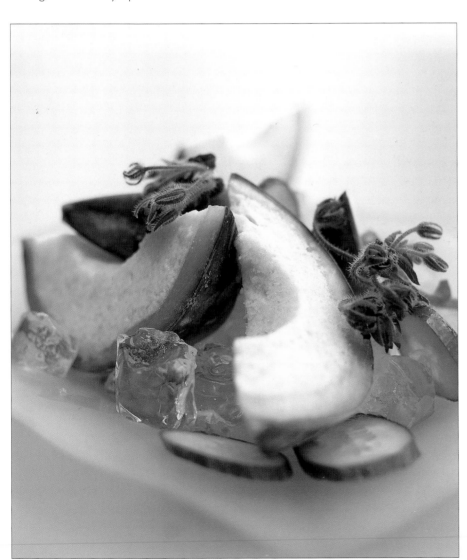

FRAGRANT FRUIT SALAD

Organic summer fruits make a delicious seasonal fruit salad. Any combination of fruits can be used, although this exotic choice is particularly suitable for a dinner party.

SERVES SIX

130g/4½oz/scant ¾ cup unrefined sugar
    or rapadura
thinly pared rind and juice of 1 lime
60ml/4 tbsp brandy
5ml/1 tsp instant coffee granules or powder
    dissolved in 30ml/2 tbsp boiling water
1 small pineapple
1 papaya
2 pomegranates
1 medium mango
2 passion fruits or kiwi fruit
fine strips of lime peel, to decorate

COOK'S TIP

Allow the salad to stand at room temperature for an hour before serving so the flavours can blend.

1 Put the sugar and lime rind in a small pan with 150ml/¼ pint/⅔ cup water. Heat gently until the sugar dissolves, then bring to the boil and simmer for 5 minutes. Leave to cool, then strain into a large serving bowl, discarding the lime rind. Stir in the lime juice, brandy and dissolved coffee.

2 Using a sharp knife, cut the plume and stalk ends from the pineapple. Peel and cut the flesh into bitesize pieces. Add to the bowl. Discard the central core.

3 Halve the papaya and scoop out the seeds. Cut away the skin, then slice the papaya. Halve the pomegranates and scoop out the seeds. Add to the bowl.

4 Cut the mango lengthways into three pieces, along each side of the stone. Peel the skin off the flesh. Cut into chunks and add to the bowl.

5 Halve the passion fruits and scoop out the flesh using a teaspoon or peel and chop the kiwi fruit. Add to the bowl and serve, decorated with lime peel.

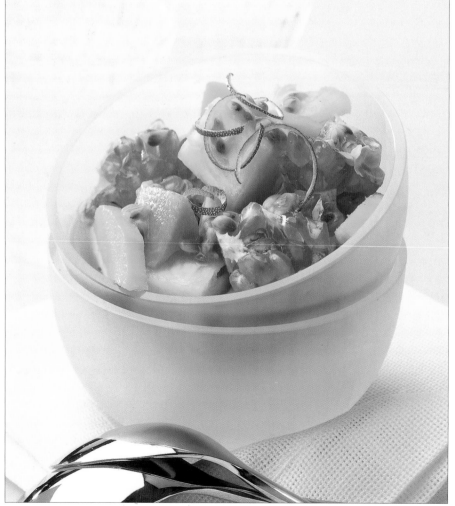

ROASTED GARLIC and SQUASH SOUP

This is a wonderful, richly flavoured dish. A spoonful of hot and spicy tomato salsa gives
bite to this sweet-tasting butternut squash and garlic soup.

SERVES FOUR TO FIVE

2 garlic bulbs, outer papery
    skin removed
75ml/5 tbsp olive oil
a few fresh thyme sprigs
I large butternut squash, halved
    and seeded
2 onions, chopped
5ml/I tsp ground coriander
1.2 litres/2 pints/5 cups vegetable or
    chicken stock
30–45ml/2–3 tbsp chopped fresh oregano
    or marjoram
sea salt and ground black pepper

For the salsa
4 large ripe tomatoes, halved and seeded
I red (bell) pepper, halved and seeded
I large fresh red chilli, halved and seeded
30–45ml/2–3 tbsp extra virgin olive oil
I5ml/I tbsp balsamic vinegar

I Preheat the oven to 220°C/425°F/
Gas 7. Place the garlic bulbs on a piece
of foil and pour over half the olive oil.
Add the thyme sprigs, then fold the foil
around the garlic bulbs to enclose them
completely. Place the foil parcel on a
baking sheet with the butternut squash
and brush the squash with I5ml/I tbsp
of the remaining olive oil. Add the
halved and seeded tomatoes, red pepper
and fresh chilli for the salsa.

2 Roast the vegetables for 25 minutes,
then remove the tomatoes, pepper and
chilli. Reduce the temperature to I90°C/
375°F/Gas 5 and cook the squash and
garlic for 20–25 minutes more, or until
the squash is tender.

3 Heat the remaining oil in a large,
heavy pan and cook the onions and
ground coriander gently for about
10 minutes, or until softened.

4 Skin the pepper and chilli and process
in a food processor or blender with the
tomatoes and 30ml/2 tbsp olive oil. Stir
in the vinegar and seasoning to taste.
Add the remaining oil if you think the
salsa needs it.

5 Squeeze the roasted garlic out of its
papery skin into the onions. Scoop the
squash out of its skin and add it to the
pan. Add the vegetable or chicken stock,
2.5ml/½ tsp salt and plenty of black
pepper. Bring to the boil and simmer for
10 minutes.

6 Stir in half the chopped fresh oregano
or marjoram and allow the soup to
cool slightly, then process it in batches
if necessary, in a food processor or
blender until smooth. Alternatively, press
the soup through a fine sieve.

7 Reheat the soup in a clean pan
without allowing it to boil, then taste for
seasoning before ladling it into individual
warmed bowls. Top each with a spoonful
of the tomato salsa and sprinkle over the
remaining chopped fresh oregano or
marjoram. Serve immediately.

FLORETS POLONAISE

Simple steamed organic vegetables become something very special with this pretty egg topping. They make a perfect dinner party side dish or are great with a weekday supper.

SERVES SIX

500g/1¼lb mixed vegetables,
    such as cauliflower, broccoli,
    romanesco and calabrese
50g/2oz/¼ cup butter or 60ml/4 tbsp extra
    virgin olive oil
finely grated rind of ½ lemon
1 large garlic clove, crushed
25g/1oz/½ cup fresh breadcrumbs, lightly
    baked or grilled (broiled) until crisp
2 eggs, hard-boiled
sea salt and ground black pepper

VARIATION

Use wholemeal (whole-wheat) breadcrumbs
instead of the white crumbs. They will give
a nuttier flavour and crunchier texture.

1 Trim the vegetables and break into
equal-size florets. Place the florets in a
steamer over a pan of boiling water and
steam for 5–7 minutes, until just tender.

2 Toss the steamed vegetables in butter
or oil and transfer to a serving dish.

3 While the vegetables are cooking, mix
together the lemon rind, garlic, seasoning
and baked or grilled breadcrumbs. Finely
chop the eggs and mix together with
the remaining ingredients. Sprinkle the
chopped egg mixture over the cooked
vegetables and serve immediately.

ORANGE CANDIED SWEET POTATOES

Organic sweet potatoes are free of the fungicides sprayed on non-organic tubers and are an excellent source of nutrients, including cancer-preventing betacarotene.

SERVES EIGHT

900g/2lb sweet potatoes
250ml/8fl oz/1 cup orange juice
50ml/2fl oz/¼ cup maple syrup
5ml/1 tsp freshly grated root ginger
7.5ml/1½ tsp ground cinnamon
6.5ml/1¼ tsp ground cardamom
2.5ml/½ tsp salt
ground black pepper
ground cinnamon and orange segments,
   to garnish

COOK'S TIP

This popular American dish is traditionally served with roast turkey at Thanksgiving and Christmas. Serve with extra orange segments to make it really special.

1 Preheat the oven to 180°C/350°F/ Gas 4. Peel and dice the potatoes and then steam them for 5 minutes.

2 Meanwhile, stir the remaining ingredients together. Spread out on to a non-stick shallow baking tin (pan).

3 Scatter the potatoes over the baking tin. Cook for 1 hour, stirring every 15 minutes, until they are tender and well coated in the spicy syrup.

4 Serve garnished with orange segments and ground cinnamon.

GARLIC CHIVE RICE with MUSHROOMS

A wide range of organic mushrooms is readily available. They combine well with rice and garlic chives to make a tasty accompaniment to vegetarian dishes, fish or chicken.

SERVES FOUR

350g/12oz/generous 1¾ cups
    long grain rice
60ml/4 tbsp groundnut (peanut) oil
1 small onion, finely chopped
2 green chillies, seeded and finely chopped
25g/1oz garlic chives, chopped
15g/½oz fresh coriander (cilantro)
600ml/1 pint/2½ cups vegetable or
    mushroom stock
2.5ml/½ tsp sea salt
250g/9oz mixed mushrooms, thickly sliced
50g/2oz cashew nuts, fried in 15ml/1 tbsp
    olive oil until golden brown
ground black pepper

1 Wash and drain the rice. Heat half the oil in a pan and cook the onion and chillies over a gentle heat, stirring occasionally, for 10–12 minutes until soft.

2 Set half the garlic chives aside. Cut the stalks off the coriander and set the leaves aside. Purée the remaining chives and the coriander stalks with the stock in a food processor or blender.

VARIATION

For a higher-fibre alternative make this dish with brown rice. Increase the cooking time in step 3 to 25–30 minutes or follow the packet instructions.

3 Add the rice to the onions and fry over a low heat, stirring frequently, for 4–5 minutes. Pour in the stock mixture, then stir in the salt and a good grinding of black pepper. Bring to the boil, then stir and reduce the heat to very low. Cover tightly with a lid and cook for 15–20 minutes, or until the rice has absorbed all the liquid.

4 Remove the pan from the heat and lay a clean, folded dishtowel over the pan, under the lid, and press on the lid to wedge it firmly in place. Leave the rice to stand for a further 10 minutes, allowing the towel to absorb the steam while the rice becomes completely tender.

5 Meanwhile, heat the remaining oil in a frying pan and cook the mushrooms for 5–6 minutes until tender and browned. Add the remaining garlic chives and cook for another 1–2 minutes.

6 Stir the cooked mushroom and chive mixture and chopped coriander leaves into the rice. Adjust the seasoning to taste, then transfer to a warmed serving dish and serve immediately, scattered with the fried cashew nuts.

SPICY VENISON CASSEROLE

Being high in flavour but low in saturated fat, organic venison is a good choice for healthy, yet rich, casseroles. Cranberries and orange bring a delicious fruitiness to this spicy recipe.

SERVES FOUR

15ml/1 tbsp olive oil
1 onion, chopped
2 celery sticks, sliced
10ml/2 tsp ground allspice
15ml/1 tbsp plain (all-purpose) or
    wholemeal (whole-wheat) flour
675g/1½lb stewing venison, cubed
225g/8oz fresh or frozen cranberries
grated rind and juice of 1 orange
900ml/1½ pints/3¾ cups beef or
    venison stock
sea salt and ground black pepper

1 Heat the oil in a flameproof casserole. Add the onion and celery and fry for about 5 minutes, or until softened.

2 Meanwhile, mix the ground allspice with the flour and either spread the mixture out on a large plate or place in a large plastic bag. Toss a few pieces of venison at a time (to prevent them becoming soggy) in the flour mixture until they are all lightly coated. Spread the floured venison out on a large plate until ready to cook.

3 When the onion and celery are just softened, remove them from the casserole using a slotted spoon and set aside. Add the venison pieces to the casserole in batches and cook until well browned and sealed on all sides.

COOK'S TIP
Freshly made home-made stock is always best, but if you are short of time, look for cartons or tubs of fresh stock in the chilled food cabinets of organic stores.

4 Add the cranberries and the orange rind and juice to the casserole along with the stock and stir well. Return the vegetables and the browned venison to the casserole and heat until simmering. Cover tightly and reduce the heat.

5 Simmer for about 45 minutes, or until the venison is tender, stirring occasionally. Season the venison casserole to taste with a little salt and plenty of ground black pepper before serving.

VARIATIONS
Farmed organic venison is increasingly easy to find and is available from many good butchers and organic meat delivery companies. It makes a rich and flavourful stew, but lean pork or braising steak could be used in place of the venison, if you prefer. You could also replace the cranberries with pitted and halved prunes and, for extra flavour, use either ale or stout instead of about half the stock.

SALMON and RICE GRATIN

This all-in-one supper dish is ideal for informal autumn entertaining as it can be made in advance and reheated for about half an hour before being served with a tossed salad.

4 Remove the pan from the heat and, without lifting the lid, allow the rice to stand, undisturbed, for 5 minutes.

5 Meanwhile, make the sauce. Mix the milk, flour and butter or margarine in a pan. Bring to the boil over a low heat, whisking constantly until the sauce is smooth and thick. Stir in the curry paste with salt and pepper to taste. Simmer for 2 minutes.

6 Preheat the grill (broiler). Remove the sauce from the heat and stir in the chopped parsley and rice, with half the cheese. Using a large metal spoon, fold in the flaked fish and eggs. Spoon into a shallow gratin dish and sprinkle with the rest of the cheese. Cook under the grill until the topping is golden brown and bubbling. Serve in individual dishes, garnished with chopped parsley.

SERVES SIX

675g/1½lb fresh salmon fillet, skinned
1 bay leaf
a few parsley stalks
1 litre/1¾ pints/4 cups water
400g/14oz/2 cups basmati rice, soaked
    and drained
30–45ml/2–3 tbsp chopped fresh parsley,
    plus extra to garnish
175g/6oz/1½ cups grated Cheddar cheese
3 hard-boiled eggs, chopped
sea salt and ground black pepper

For the sauce
1 litre/1¾ pints/4 cups milk or soya milk
40g/1½oz/⅓ cup plain (all-purpose) flour
40g/1½oz/3 tbsp butter or
    non-hydrogenated margarine
5ml/1 tsp mild curry paste

1 Put the salmon fillet in a wide, shallow pan. Add the bay leaf and parsley stalks, with a little salt and plenty of black pepper. Pour in the water and bring to simmering point. Poach the fish for about 12 minutes until just tender.

2 Lift the salmon fillet out of the pan using a slotted spoon, then strain the cooking liquid into a large pan. Leave the fish to cool, then remove any visible bones and flake the flesh gently into bitesize pieces with a fork.

3 Add the soaked and drained rice to the pan containing the fish-poaching liquid. Bring the liquid to the boil, then lower the heat, cover tightly with a lid and simmer gently for 10 minutes without lifting the lid.

VARIATIONS
Organically farmed prawns (shrimp) could be substituted for the salmon, and other hard cheeses, such as Gruyère or Red Leicester, could be used instead of the Cheddar cheese.

POTATO-TOPPED FISH PIE

This traditional Scottish dish should be prepared from wild fish such as hoki, caught sustainably. Always ensure you buy wild fish bearing the MSC logo.

SERVES FOUR

675g/1½lb hoki fillets (or other sustainably caught white fish)
300ml/½ pint/1¼ cups milk or soya milk
½ lemon, sliced
1 bay leaf
1 fresh thyme sprig
4–5 black peppercorns
50g/2oz/¼ cup butter or non-hydrogenated margarine
25g/1oz/¼ cup plain (all-purpose) flour
30ml/2 tbsp chopped fresh parsley
5ml/1 tsp anchovy essence
150g/5oz/2 cups shiitake or chestnut mushrooms, sliced
sea salt, ground black pepper and cayenne pepper

For the topping
450g/1lb potatoes, cooked and mashed with milk or soya milk
50g/2oz/¼ cup butter or non-hydrogenated margarine
2 tomatoes, sliced
25g/1oz/¼ cup grated Cheddar cheese

1 Put the fish skin side down in a shallow pan. Add the milk, lemon slices, bay leaf, thyme and peppercorns. Bring to the boil, then lower the heat and poach gently for about 5 minutes until just cooked. Strain off and reserve the milk. Remove the fish skin and flake the flesh, discarding any bones.

2 Melt half the butter in a small pan, stir in the flour and cook gently for 1 minute. Add the reserved milk and boil, whisking, until smooth and creamy. Stir in the parsley and anchovy essence and season to taste.

3 Heat the remaining butter in a frying pan, add the sliced mushrooms and sauté until tender. Season and add to the flaked fish. Mix the sauce into the fish and stir gently to combine. Transfer the mixture to an ovenproof casserole.

4 Preheat the oven to 200°C/400°F/ Gas 6. Beat the mashed potato with the butter until very creamy. Season, then spread the topping evenly over the fish. Fork up the surface and arrange the sliced tomatoes around the edge. Sprinkle the exposed topping with the grated cheese.

5 Bake for 20–25 minutes until the topping is browned. If you prefer, finish the browning under a hot grill (broiler).

VARIATION
Instead of using plain mashed potatoes, try a mixture of mashed potato and mashed swede (rutabaga) or sweet potato.

GRILLED MACKEREL with SPICY DHAL

Oily fish such as mackerel are nutritious and great for your nervous system. They are complemented by a tart or sour accompaniment, like these delicious tamarind-flavoured lentils or split peas. Serve with chopped fresh tomatoes, onion salad and flat bread.

SERVES FOUR

250g/9oz/generous I cup red lentils, or
   yellow split peas (soaked overnight)
I litre/1¾ pints/4 cups water
30ml/2 tbsp sunflower oil
2.5ml/½ tsp each mustard seeds,
   cumin seeds, fennel seeds and
   fenugreek or cardamom seeds
5ml/I tsp ground turmeric
3–4 dried red chillies, crumbled
30ml/2 tbsp tamarind paste
30ml/2 tbsp chopped fresh coriander
   (cilantro)
4 mackerels
ground black pepper
fresh red chilli slices and finely chopped
   coriander, to garnish
flat bread and tomatoes, to serve

I Rinse the lentils or split peas, drain them thoroughly and put them in a pan. Pour in the water and bring to the boil. Lower the heat, partially cover the pan and simmer the lentils or split peas for 30–40 minutes, stirring occasionally, until they are tender and mushy.

2 Heat the oil in a wok or shallow pan. Add the mustard seeds, then cover and cook for a few seconds until they pop. Remove the lid, add the rest of the seeds, with the turmeric and chillies and fry for a few more seconds.

3 Stir in the lentils or split peas and the tamarind paste and mix well. Bring to the boil, then simmer for 10 minutes until thick. Stir in the coriander.

4 Clean the fish then heat a ridged griddle or the grill (broiler) until very hot. Make six diagonal slashes on either side of each fish and remove the head. Season, then grill for 5–7 minutes on each side. Serve, garnished with red chilli and chopped coriander, accompanied by the dhal, flat bread and tomatoes.

SOLE with WILD MUSHROOMS

If possible, use organic chanterelles for this dish; their glowing orange colour combines really wonderfully with the intensely golden sauce. Otherwise, use any pale-coloured or oyster mushrooms that you can find instead.

SERVES FOUR

4 Dover sole fillets, about 115g/4oz
   each, skinned
50g/2oz/¼ cup butter or
   non-hydrogenated margarine
500ml/17fl oz/generous 2 cups fish stock
150g/5oz/2 cups chanterelles or
   oyster mushrooms
a large pinch of saffron threads
150ml/¼ pint/⅔ cup double (heavy) cream
   or soya cream
1 egg yolk
sea salt and ground white pepper
flat leaf parsley sprigs, to garnish
boiled new potatoes and steamed broccoli
   florets, to serve

1 Preheat the oven to 200°C/400°F/ Gas 6. Cut the sole fillets in half lengthways and place them on a board with the skinned side uppermost. Season, then roll them up. Use a little of the butter to grease a baking dish just large enough to hold all the sole fillets in a single layer. Arrange the rolls in it, then pour over the fish stock. Cover tightly with foil and bake for 12–15 minutes until cooked through.

2 Meanwhile, pick off any bits of fern or twig from the chanterelles and wipe the mushrooms with a damp cloth. Halve or quarter any large ones. Heat the remaining butter in a frying pan until foaming and sauté the mushrooms for 3–4 minutes until just tender. Season with salt and pepper and keep hot.

3 Lift the cooked sole fillets out of the cooking liquid and place them on a heated serving dish. Keep hot. Strain the liquid into a small pan, add the saffron, set over a very high heat and boil until reduced to about 250ml/8fl oz/1 cup. Stir in the cream and let the sauce bubble gently for a few seconds.

4 Lightly beat the egg yolk in a small bowl, pour on a little of the hot sauce and stir well. Stir the mixture into the remaining sauce in the pan and cook over a very low heat for 1–2 minutes until slightly thickened. Season to taste. Stir the chanterelles into the sauce and pour it over the sole fillets. Garnish with parsley sprigs and serve at once. Boiled new potatoes and steamed broccoli florets make the perfect accompaniment.

STICKY PEAR PUDDING

Pears are at their best in autumn and, combined with other organic ingredients such as cloves, coffee and maple syrup, they form the basis of this indulgent dessert.

SERVES SIX

30ml/2 tbsp ground coffee
15ml/1 tbsp near-boiling water
4 ripe pears
juice of ½ orange
50g/2oz/½ cup toasted hazelnuts
115g/4oz/½ cup butter or
    non-hydrogenated margarine, softened
115g/4oz/generous ½ cup unrefined caster
    (superfine) sugar or rapadura, plus an
    extra 15ml/1 tbsp for baking
2 eggs, beaten
50g/2oz/½ cup self-raising (self-rising)
    flour, sifted
pinch of ground cloves
8 whole cloves (optional)
45ml/3 tbsp maple syrup
fine strips of orange rind, to decorate

For the orange cream
300ml/½ pint/1¼ cups whipping cream
15ml/1 tbsp unrefined icing
    (confectioners') sugar, sifted
finely grated rind of ½ orange

1 Preheat the oven to 180°C/350°F/ Gas 4. Lightly grease a 20cm/8in loose-based sandwich tin (shallow cake pan). Put the ground coffee in a small bowl and pour the water over. Leave to infuse for 4 minutes, then strain through a fine sieve.

VARIATION

Apple and cinnamon could be used in this pudding instead of pears and cloves, with a lemon cream in place of orange cream.

2 Peel, halve and core the pears. Thinly slice across the pear halves part of the way through. Brush the pears with orange juice. Grind the hazelnuts in a coffee grinder until fine.

3 Beat the butter and the caster sugar together until very light and fluffy. Gradually beat in the eggs, then fold in the flour, ground cloves, hazelnuts and coffee.

4 Spoon the mixture into the prepared sandwich tin and level the surface with a spatula.

5 Pat the pears dry on kitchen paper, then arrange them carefully in the sponge mixture, flat side down.

6 Lightly press two whole cloves, if using, into each pear half. Brush the pears with 15ml/1 tbsp maple syrup.

7 Sprinkle 15ml/1 tbsp caster sugar over the pears. Bake for 45–50 minutes, or until firm and well-risen.

8 While the sponge is cooking, make the orange cream. Whip the cream, icing sugar and orange rind until soft peaks form. Spoon into a serving dish and chill until needed.

9 Allow the sponge to cool for about 10 minutes in the tin, then remove and place on a serving plate. Lightly brush with the remaining maple syrup before decorating with orange rind and serving warm with the orange cream.

COOK'S TIP

Organic pears are a good source of soluble fibre and are great at lowering cholesterol and easing constipation. Buy slightly underripe fruit and leave them to ripen on a sunny windowsill for a few days – overripe pears go off quickly.

BAKED APPLE DUMPLINGS

A wonderful way to make the most of apples in season. The sharpness of the fruit contrasts perfectly with the maple syrup drizzled over this delightful pastry parcel.

SERVES EIGHT

8 firm cooking apples, peeled
1 egg white
130g/4½oz/⅔ cup unrefined caster
    (superfine) sugar or rapadura
45ml/3 tbsp double (heavy) cream or
    soya cream, plus extra whipped cream,
    to serve
2.5ml/½ tsp vanilla essence (extract)
250ml/8fl oz/1 cup maple syrup

For the pastry
475g/1lb 2oz/4½ cups plain
    (all-purpose) flour
350g/12oz/1½ cups butter or
    non-hydrogenated margarine, diced

1 To make the pastry, sift the flour into a large bowl. Rub in the butter until the mixture resembles fine breadcrumbs.

2 Sprinkle over 175ml/6fl oz/¾ cup water and mix until the dough holds together, adding more water if necessary. Gather into a ball. Wrap in clear film (plastic wrap) and chill for 10 minutes. Preheat the oven to 220°C/425°F/Gas 7.

3 Cutting from the stem end, core the apples without cutting through the base. Roll out the pastry thinly. Cut squares almost large enough to enclose the apples; brush with egg white and set an apple in the centre of each.

4 Cut pastry rounds to cover the tops of the cored apples. Reserve the pastry trimmings. Combine the unrefined sugar, cream and vanilla essence in a small bowl. Spoon one-eighth of the mixture into the hollow of each apple.

5 Place a pastry round on top of each apple, then bring up the sides of the pastry square to enclose it, pleating the larger piece of pastry to make a snug fit around the apple. Moisten the joins with cold water where they overlap and press down so they stick in place.

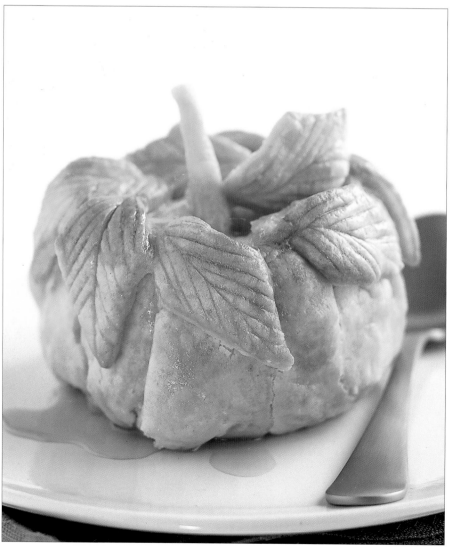

6 Make apple stalks and leaves from the pastry trimmings and use to decorate the dumplings. Set them in a large greased baking dish, at least 2cm/¾in apart. Bake for 30 minutes, then reduce the oven temperature to 180°C/350°F/Gas 4 and continue baking for 20 minutes more, or until the pastry is golden brown and the apples are tender.

7 Transfer the dumplings to a serving dish. Mix the maple syrup with the juices in the baking dish and drizzle over the dumplings. Serve the dumplings hot with whipped cream.

HOT BLACKBERRY and APPLE SOUFFLÉS

*The deliciously tart autumn flavours of blackberry and apple complement each other
perfectly to make a light, mouthwatering hot pudding.*

MAKES SIX

butter or non-hydrogenated margarine,
    for greasing
150g/5oz/¾ cup unrefined caster (superfine)
    sugar or rapadura, plus extra for dusting
350g/12oz/3 cups blackberries
I large cooking apple, peeled and finely diced
grated rind and juice of I orange
3 egg whites
unrefined icing (confectioner's) sugar,
    for dusting

I Preheat the oven to 200°C/400°F/
Gas 6. Generously grease six 150ml/
¼ pint/⅔ cup individual soufflé dishes
with butter and dust with caster sugar,
shaking out the excess sugar.

2 Put a baking sheet in the oven to heat.
Cook the blackberries, diced apple and
orange rind and juice in a pan for about
10 minutes or until the apple has pulped
down well. Press through a sieve into a
bowl. Stir in 50g/2oz/¼ cup of the caster
sugar. Set aside to cool.

3 Put a spoonful of the fruit purée into
each prepared soufflé dish and spread
evenly. Set the dishes aside.

4 Place the egg whites in a grease-free
bowl and whisk until they form stiff
peaks. Very gradually whisk in the
remaining caster sugar to make a stiff,
glossy meringue mixture.

5 Fold in the remaining fruit purée and
spoon the flavoured meringue into the
prepared dishes. Level the tops with a
palette knife, and run a table knife
around the edge of each dish.

6 Place the dishes on the hot baking
sheet and bake for 10–15 minutes until
the soufflés have risen well and are
lightly browned. Dust the tops with
icing sugar and serve immediately.

COOK'S TIP
Running a table knife around the inside
edge of the soufflé dishes before baking
helps the soufflés to rise evenly without
sticking to the rim of the dish.

PARSNIP CAKE with ORANGE ICING

This fabulous vegan cake is similar to the ever-popular carrot cake, but uses non-dairy alternatives to margarine and cream cheese.

SERVES TEN

250g/9oz/2¼ cups wholemeal (whole-wheat) self-raising (self-rising) flour
15ml/1 tbsp baking powder
5ml/1 tsp ground cinnamon
5ml/1 tsp freshly ground nutmeg
130g/4½oz/9 tbsp vegan margarine
130g/4½oz/scant ½ cup unrefined soft light brown sugar or rapadura
250g/9oz parsnips, coarsely grated
1 banana, mashed
finely grated rind and juice of 1 orange

For the topping
225g/8oz/1 cup organic soya cream cheese
45ml/3 tbsp unrefined icing (confectioner's) sugar
juice of 1 small orange
fine strips of orange peel

1 Preheat the oven to 180°C/350°F/ Gas 4. Lightly grease and line the base of a 900g/2lb loaf tin (pan).

2 Sift the flour, baking powder and spices into a large bowl. Add any bran remaining in the sieve.

COOK'S TIP
If you can't find self-raising wholemeal flour, use ordinary wholemeal flour and add an extra 15ml/1 tbsp baking powder.

VARIATION
Serve the cake as a dessert with a generous spoonful of organic natural (plain) yogurt, crème fraîche or soya cream, flavoured with grated orange rind or a little Calvados.

3 Melt the margarine in a pan, add the sugar and stir until dissolved. Make a well in the flour mixture, then add the melted margarine and sugar. Mix in the parsnips, banana and orange rind and juice. Spoon the mixture into the prepared tin and level the top with the back of a spoon.

4 Bake for 45–50 minutes until a skewer inserted into the centre of the cake comes out clean. Allow the cake to cool slightly before removing from the tin, then transfer to a wire rack to cool completely.

5 To make the topping, beat together the cream cheese, icing sugar, orange juice and strips of orange peel until smooth. Spread the topping evenly over the cake.

COUNTRY APPLE CAKE

This perennial favourite is a great way to take advantage of the season's apple harvest. There are any number of organic apples available nowadays, including heirloom and almost-lost local varieties, which makes cooking and eating this cake a real treat.

MAKES ONE 18CM/7IN CAKE

115g/4oz/½ cup soft non-hydrogenated
   margarine
115g/4oz/½ cup unrefined soft light brown
   sugar or rapadura
2 eggs, beaten
115g/4oz/1 cup self-raising (self-rising)
   flour, sifted
50g/2oz/½ cup rice flour
5ml/1 tsp baking powder
10ml/2 tsp mixed (apple-pie) spice
1 cooking apple, cored and chopped
115g/4oz/scant 1 cup raisins
about 60ml/4 tbsp milk or soya milk
15g/½oz/2 tbsp flaked (sliced) almonds

1 Preheat the oven to 160°C/325°F/ Gas 3. Lightly grease and line a deep 18cm/ 7in round, loose-bottomed cake tin (pan).

2 Cream the margarine and sugar in a mixing bowl. Gradually add the eggs, then fold in the flours, baking powder and spice.

3 Stir in the chopped apple, raisins and enough of the milk to make a soft, dropping consistency.

4 Turn the mixture into the prepared tin and level the surface. Sprinkle the flaked almonds over the top. Bake the cake for 1–1¼ hours until risen, firm to the touch and golden brown.

5 Cool the apple cake in the tin for about 10 minutes, then turn out on to a wire rack to cool. Cut into slices when cold. Alternatively, serve the cake warm, in slices, with custard or ice cream. Store the cold cake in an airtight container or wrapped in foil.

VARIATIONS
• Use sultanas (golden raisins) or chopped dried apricots or pears instead of the raisins.
• A wide variety of organic ice creams is available from independent dairies and supermarkets – vanilla goes particularly well with this cake.

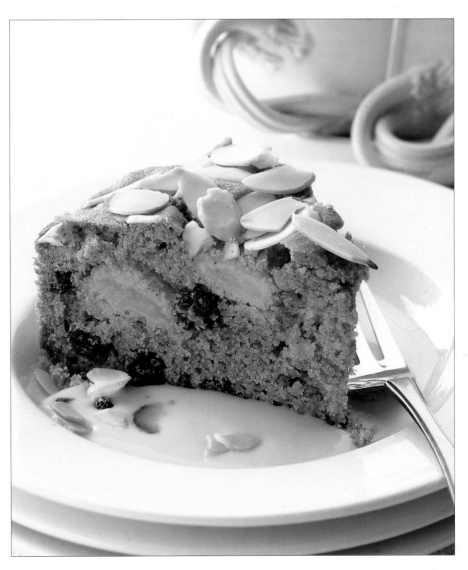

OAT and RAISIN DROP SCONES

Serve these easy-to-make organic scones at tea time or as a dessert – or even a special breakfast or brunch – with real maple syrup or clear honey.

MAKES ABOUT SIXTEEN

75g/3oz/⅔ cup self-raising (self-rising) flour
2.5ml/½ tsp baking powder
50g/2oz/scant ½ cup raisins
25g/1oz/¼ cup fine oatmeal
25g/1oz/2 tbsp unrefined caster (superfine) sugar or rapadura
grated rind of 1 orange
2 egg yolks
10g/¼oz/½ tbsp unsalted (sweet) butter or non-hydrogenated margarine, melted
200ml/7fl oz/scant 1 cup single (light) cream or soya cream
200ml/7fl oz/scant 1 cup water
sunflower oil, for greasing
icing (confectioner's) sugar, for dusting

1 Sift the self-raising flour and baking powder together into a large mixing bowl.

COOK'S TIP
Wrap the cooked scones in a clean dishtowel to keep them soft.

2 Add the raisins, oatmeal, sugar and orange rind. Gradually beat in the egg yolks, butter, cream and water to make a creamy batter.

3 Lightly grease and heat a large heavy frying pan or griddle and drop about 30ml/2 tbsp of batter at a time on to the pan or griddle to make six or seven small pancakes.

4 Cook over a moderate heat until bubbles show on the scones' surface, then turn them over and cook for a further 2 minutes until golden.

5 Transfer to a plate and dust with icing sugar. Keep warm while cooking the remaining mixture. Serve warm.

BARLEY RISOTTO with ROASTED SQUASH and LEEKS

This is more like a pilaff made with slightly chewy, nutty-flavoured pearl barley than a classic risotto. Sweet organic leeks and roasted squash are superb with this earthy grain.

SERVES FOUR TO FIVE

200g/7oz/1 cup pearl barley
1 butternut squash, peeled, seeded and
    cut into chunks
10ml/2 tsp chopped fresh thyme
60ml/4 tbsp olive oil
25g/1oz/2 tbsp butter
4 leeks, cut into fairly thick diagonal slices
2 garlic cloves, finely chopped
175g/6oz/2½ cups chestnut mushrooms, sliced
2 carrots, coarsely grated
about 120ml/4fl oz/½ cup vegetable stock
30ml/2 tbsp chopped fresh flat leaf parsley
50g/2oz/⅔ cup Parmesan cheese or
    premium Italian-style vegetarian cheese,
    grated or shaved
45ml/3 tbsp pumpkin seeds, toasted, or
    chopped walnuts
sea salt and ground black pepper

1 Rinse the barley, then cook it in simmering water, keeping the pan part-covered, for 35–45 minutes, or until tender. Drain. Preheat the oven to 200°C/400°F/Gas 6.

2 Place the squash in a roasting pan with half the thyme. Season with pepper and toss with half the oil. Roast, stirring once, for 30–35 minutes, until the squash is tender and beginning to brown.

3 Heat half the butter with the remaining olive oil in a large frying pan. Cook the leeks and garlic gently for 5 minutes. Add the mushrooms and remaining thyme, then cook until the liquid from the mushrooms evaporates and they begin to fry.

4 Stir in the carrots and cook for about 2 minutes, then add the barley and most of the vegetable stock. Season well and part-cover the pan. Cook for a further 5 minutes. Pour in the remaining stock if the mixture seems dry.

5 Stir in the parsley, the remaining butter and half the cheese, then stir in the squash. Add seasoning to taste and serve immediately, sprinkled with the toasted pumpkin seeds or walnuts and the remaining cheese.

VARIATIONS
• Make the risotto with organic brown rice instead of the barley – cook following the packet instructions and continue from step 2.
• Any type of organic mushrooms can be used in this recipe – try sliced field (portabello) mushrooms for a hearty flavour.

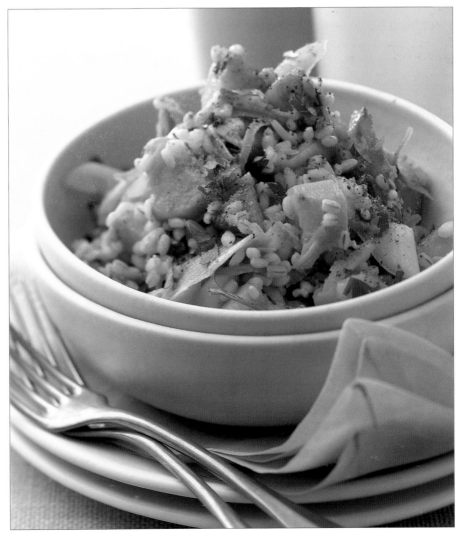

PEPPERS FILLED with SPICED VEGETABLES

Indian spices season the potato and aubergine stuffing in these colourful baked peppers.
They are good with brown rice and a lentil dhal. Alternatively, serve them with a salad,
Indian breads and a cucumber or mint and yogurt raita.

SERVES SIX

6 large evenly shaped red or
    yellow (bell) peppers
500g/1¼lb waxy potatoes
1 small onion, chopped
4–5 garlic cloves, chopped
5cm/2in piece fresh root ginger, chopped
1–2 fresh green chillies, seeded
    and chopped
105ml/7 tbsp water
90–105ml/6–7 tbsp sunflower oil
1 aubergine (eggplant), diced
10ml/2 tsp cumin seeds
5ml/1 tsp kalonji seeds
2.5ml/½ tsp ground turmeric
5ml/1 tsp ground coriander
5ml/1 tsp ground toasted cumin seeds
pinch of cayenne pepper
about 30ml/2 tbsp lemon juice
sea salt and ground black pepper
30ml/2 tbsp chopped fresh coriander
    (cilantro), to garnish

1 Cut the tops off the red or yellow peppers, then remove and discard the seeds. Cut a thin slice off the base of the peppers, if necessary, to make them stand upright.

2 Bring a large pan of lightly salted water to the boil. Add the peppers and cook for 5–6 minutes. Drain and leave them upside down in a colander.

COOK'S TIP
The hottest part of a chilli is the white membrane that connects the seeds to the flesh. Removing the seeds and membrane before cooking gives a milder flavour.

3 Cook the potatoes in lightly salted, boiling water for 10–12 minutes until just tender. Drain, cool and peel, then cut into 1cm/½in dice.

4 Put the onion, garlic, ginger and green chillies in a food processor or blender with 60ml/4 tbsp of the water and process to a purée.

5 Heat 45ml/3 tbsp of the sunflower oil in a large, deep frying pan and cook the diced aubergine, stirring occasionally, until it is evenly browned on all sides. Remove from the pan and set aside. Add another 30ml/2 tbsp of the sunflower oil to the pan, add the diced potatoes and cook until lightly browned on all sides. Remove the potatoes from the pan and set aside.

6 If necessary, add another 15ml/1 tbsp sunflower oil to the pan, then add the cumin and kalonji seeds. Fry briefly until the seeds darken, then add the turmeric, coriander and ground cumin. Cook for 15 seconds. Stir in the onion and garlic purée and fry, scraping the pan with a spatula, until the onions begin to brown.

7 Return the potatoes and aubergine to the pan, season with salt, pepper and 1–2 pinches of cayenne. Add the remaining water and 15ml/1 tbsp lemon juice and then cook, stirring, until the liquid evaporates. Preheat the oven to 190°C/375°F/Gas 5.

8 Fill the peppers with the spiced vegetable mixture and place on a lightly greased baking tray. Brush the peppers with a little oil and bake for 30–35 minutes until they are cooked. Allow to cool a little, then sprinkle with a little more lemon juice, garnish with the coriander and serve.

COOK'S TIP
Kalonji, or nigella as it is also known, is a tiny black seed. It is widely used in Indian cookery, especially sprinkled over breads or in potato dishes. It has a mild, slightly nutty flavour and is best toasted for a few seconds in a dry or lightly oiled frying pan over a medium heat before using in a recipe. This helps to bring out its flavour, as with most spices.

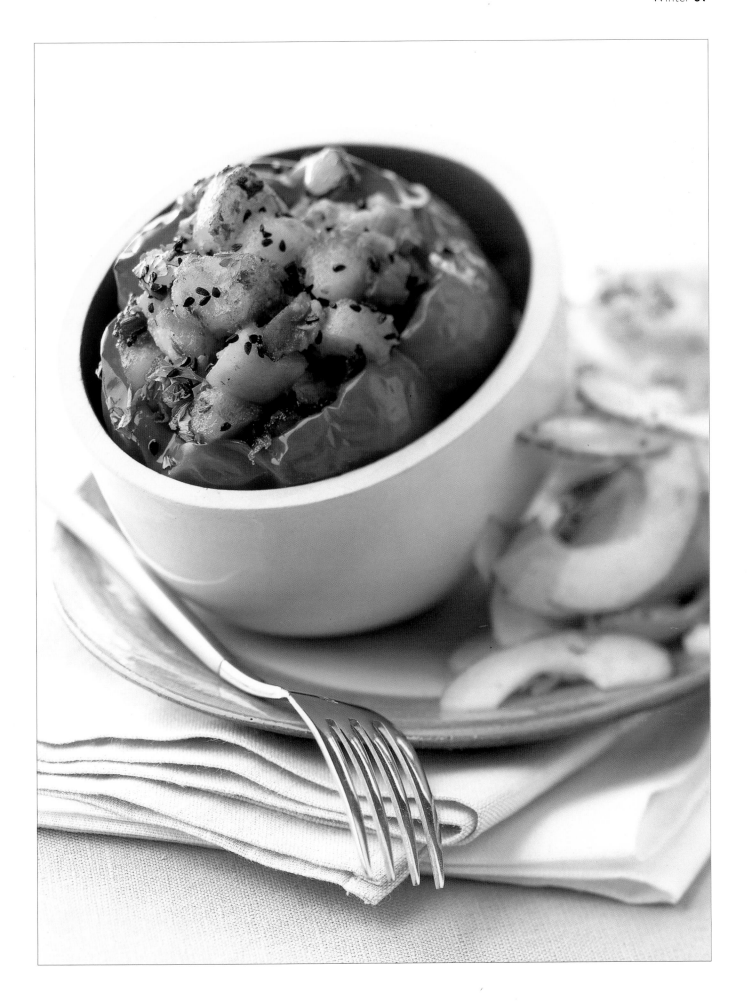

CHICKEN CASSEROLE with WINTER VEGETABLES

A casserole of wonderfully tender organic chicken, winter root vegetables and lentils, finished with crème fraîche, mustard and tarragon.

SERVES FOUR

350g/12oz onions
350g/12oz leeks
225g/8oz carrots
450g/1lb swede (rutabaga)
30ml/2 tbsp olive oil
4 chicken portions, about 900g/2lb
    total weight
115g/4oz/½ cup green lentils
475ml/16fl oz/2 cups chicken stock
300ml/½ pint/1¼ cups apple juice
10ml/2 tsp cornflour (cornstarch)
45ml/3 tbsp crème fraîche
10ml/2 tsp wholegrain mustard
30ml/2 tbsp chopped fresh tarragon
sea salt and ground black pepper
fresh tarragon sprigs, to garnish

1 Preheat the oven to 190°C/375°F/ Gas 5. Prepare and chop the vegetables.

2 Heat the oil in a large flameproof casserole. Season the chicken portions and brown them in the hot oil until golden. Remove the chicken from the pan.

3 Add the onions to the casserole and cook for 5 minutes, stirring, until they begin to soften and colour. Add the leeks, carrots, swede and lentils to the casserole and stir over a medium heat for 2 minutes.

4 Return the chicken to the pan, then add the stock, apple juice and seasoning. Bring to the boil and cover tightly. Cook in the oven for 50–60 minutes, or until the chicken and lentils are tender.

5 Place the casserole on the hob (stovetop) over a medium heat. In a small bowl, blend the cornflour with about 30ml/2 tbsp water to make a smooth paste and add to the casserole with the crème fraîche, wholegrain mustard and chopped tarragon. Adjust the seasoning, then simmer gently for about 2 minutes, stirring, until thickened slightly, before serving, garnished with tarragon sprigs.

COOK'S TIP
Chop the vegetables into similarly sized pieces so that they cook evenly. Organic vegetables do not need to be peeled.

BRAISED SHOULDER of MUTTON with PEARL BARLEY and BABY VEGETABLES

A wonderful variety of organic grains is readily available. In this tasty winter stew, pearl barley absorbs all the juices to become full-flavoured with a nutty texture when cooked.

SERVES FOUR

60ml/4 tbsp olive oil

1 large onion, chopped

2 garlic cloves, chopped

2 celery sticks, sliced

a little plain (all-purpose) or wholemeal (whole-wheat) flour

675g/1½lb boned shoulder of mutton, cut into cubes

900ml–1 litre/1½–1¾ pints/3¾–4 cups mutton stock

115g/4oz/½ cup pearl barley

225g/8oz baby carrots

225g/8oz baby turnips

sea salt and ground black pepper

30ml/2 tbsp chopped fresh marjoram, to garnish

warm, crusty bread, to serve

1 Heat 45ml/3 tbsp of the oil in a flameproof casserole. Cook the onion and garlic until softened, add the celery, then cook until the vegetables brown.

2 Season the flour and toss the mutton in it. Use a draining spoon to remove the vegetables from the casserole. Add the remaining oil to the juices in the casserole and heat. Brown the mutton in batches until golden.

3 When all the meat is browned, return it to the casserole with the vegetables. Stir in 900ml/1½ pints/3¾ cups of the stock and the pearl barley. Cover, then bring to the boil, reduce the heat and simmer for 1 hour, or until the pearl barley and mutton are tender.

4 Add the baby carrots and turnips to the casserole for the final 15 minutes of cooking. Stir the meat occasionally during cooking and add the remaining stock, if necessary. Stir in seasoning to taste, and serve piping hot, garnished with marjoram, with warm, crusty bread as an accompaniment.

CHILLI CON CARNE

Originally made with finely chopped beef, chillies and kidney beans by hungry labourers working on the Texan railroad, this famous Tex-Mex stew has become an international favourite. Be authentic by using organic ingredients.

SERVES EIGHT

1.2kg/2½lb lean braising steak
30ml/2 tbsp sunflower oil
1 large onion, chopped
2 garlic cloves, finely chopped
15ml/1 tbsp plain (all-purpose) or
   wholemeal (whole-wheat) flour
300ml/½ pint/1¼ cups red wine
300ml/½ pint/1¼ cups beef stock
30ml/2 tbsp tomato purée (paste)
sea salt and ground black pepper
fresh coriander (cilantro) leaves, to garnish
boiled white or brown rice, to serve

For the beans
30ml/2 tbsp olive oil
1 onion, chopped
1 red chilli, seeded and chopped
2 × 400g/14oz cans red kidney beans,
   drained and rinsed
400g/14oz can chopped tomatoes

For the topping
6 tomatoes, peeled and chopped
1 green chilli, seeded and chopped
30ml/2 tbsp chopped fresh chives
30ml/2 tbsp chopped fresh coriander
150ml/¼ pint/⅔ cup sour cream

1 Cut the meat into thick strips and then cut it crossways into small cubes. Heat the oil in a large, flameproof casserole. Add the chopped onion and garlic, and cook, stirring occasionally, for 5–8 minutes until softened but not coloured. Meanwhile, season the flour with a little salt and plenty of pepper and place it on a plate, then toss a batch of meat in it.

2 Use a draining spoon to remove the onion from the pan, then add the floured beef and cook over a high heat, stirring occasionally with a wooden spoon until browned on all sides. Remove from the pan and set aside, then flour and brown another batch of meat.

3 When the last batch of meat is browned, return the first batches with the onion to the pan. Stir in the wine, stock and tomato purée. Bring to the boil, reduce the heat and simmer for 45 minutes, or until the beef is tender.

4 Meanwhile, to make the beans, heat the olive oil in a frying pan and cook the onion and chilli until softened. Add the kidney beans and tomatoes and simmer gently for 20–25 minutes.

5 Mix the tomatoes, chilli, chives and coriander for the topping. Ladle the meat on to plates, then add the beans and the tomato topping. Top with sour cream and coriander leaves and serve with rice.

SMOKED HADDOCK with MUSTARD CABBAGE

A wide range of organic mustards are available – wholegrain is used in this warming winter dish, but any type can be used instead.

2 Meanwhile put the smoked haddock fillet in a large shallow pan with the milk, onion rings and bay leaves. Add the lemon slices and white peppercorns. Bring to simmering point, cover and poach until the fish flakes easily when tested with the tip of a sharp knife. This will take 8–10 minutes, depending on the thickness of the fillets. Take the pan off the heat and set aside until needed. Preheat the grill (broiler).

3 Cut the tomatoes in half horizontally, season them with a little salt and plenty of pepper and grill (broil) until lightly browned. Drain the cabbage, refresh under cold water and drain again.

4 Heat the butter or oil in a shallow pan or wok, add the cabbage and toss over the heat for 2 minutes. Mix in the mustard and season to taste, then tip the cabbage into a warmed serving dish.

SERVES FOUR

I Savoy or pointu cabbage
675g/1 ½lb undyed smoked haddock fillet
300ml/½ pint/1¼ cups milk or
    soya milk
½ onion, peeled and sliced into rings
2 bay leaves
½ lemon, sliced
4 white peppercorns
4 ripe tomatoes
50g/2oz/¼ cup butter or 50ml/3½ tbsp
    olive oil
30ml/2 tbsp wholegrain mustard
juice of I lemon
sea salt and ground black pepper
30ml/2 tbsp chopped fresh parsley,
    to garnish

I Cut the Savoy or pointu cabbage in half, remove the central core and thick ribs, then shred the cabbage. Cook in a pan of lightly salted boiling water, or steam over boiling water for about 10 minutes until just tender. Leave in the pan or steamer until required.

5 Drain the haddock. Skin and cut the fish into four pieces. Place on top of the cabbage with some of the cooked onion rings and grilled tomato halves. Pour on the lemon juice, then sprinkle with chopped fresh parsley and serve.

DRIED FRUIT COMPOTE

Compotes made with dried fruit are just as wonderful as those made with fresh fruits, especially in winter when fewer organic fresh fruit varieties are in season.

SERVES FOUR

225g/8oz/1⅓ cups mixed dried fruit
75g/3oz/⅔ cup dried cherries
75g/3oz/⅔ cup sultanas (golden raisins)
10 dried prunes
10 dried apricots
hot, freshly brewed fragrant tea, such as
 Earl Grey or jasmine, to cover
15–30ml/1–2 tbsp unrefined caster
 (superfine) sugar or rapadura
¼ lemon, sliced
60ml/4 tbsp brandy

1 Put the dried fruits in a bowl and pour over the hot tea. Add sugar to taste and the lemon slices. Cover with a plate, set aside and leave to cool to room temperature.

2 When the fruits are cool, cover the bowl with clear film (plastic wrap) and chill in the refrigerator for at least 2 hours and preferably overnight. Just before serving, pour in the brandy and stir well.

MOROCCAN RICE PUDDING

*A simple and delicious alternative to a traditional British rice pudding. The rice is cooked
in almond-flavoured milk and delicately flavoured with cinnamon and orange flower water.*

SERVES SIX

25g/1oz/¼ cup almonds, chopped
450g/1lb/2¼ cups pudding rice
25g/1oz/¼ cup unrefined icing
   (confectioners') sugar or rapadura
1 cinnamon stick
50g/2oz/¼ cup butter or
   non-hydrogenated margarine
1.5ml/¼ tsp almond essence (extract)
175ml/6fl oz/¾ cup milk or soya milk
175ml/6fl oz/¾ cup single (light) cream or
   soya cream
30ml/2 tbsp orange flower water
toasted flaked (sliced) almonds and ground
   cinnamon, to decorate

1 Put the almonds in a food processor
or blender with 60ml/4 tbsp of very hot
water. Process until the almonds are
finely chopped, then push through a
sieve into a bowl. Return the almond
mixture to the food processor or
blender, add a further 60ml/4 tbsp very
hot water, and process again. Push the
almond mixture through the sieve into
a pan.

2 Add 300ml/½ pint/1¼ cups water and
bring the mixture to the boil. Add the
rice, icing sugar or rapadura, cinnamon
stick, half the butter, the almond
essence, half the milk and half the cream.

3 Bring to the boil, then simmer,
covered, for about 30 minutes, adding
more milk and cream as the rice mixture
thickens. Continue to cook the rice,
stirring, and adding the remaining milk
and cream, until the pudding becomes
thick and creamy. Stir in the orange
flower water, then taste the rice pudding
for sweetness, adding a little extra sugar,
if necessary.

4 Pour the rice pudding into a serving
bowl and sprinkle with the toasted
flaked almonds. Dot with the remaining
butter and dust with a little ground
cinnamon. Serve the pudding hot.

PLUM CHARLOTTES with FOAMY CALVADOS SAUCE

A variety of different types of organic plums are available at this time of year – from tangy yellow greengages to sweet and juicy Victorias.

SERVES FOUR

115g/4oz/½ cup butter or
    non-hydrogenated margarine, melted
50g/2oz/¼ cup demerara (raw) sugar
    or rapadura
450g/1lb ripe plums, stoned (pitted) and
    thickly sliced
25g/1oz/2 tbsp unrefined caster (superfine)
    sugar or rapadura
30ml/2 tbsp water
1.5ml/¼ tsp ground cinnamon
25g/1oz/¼ cup ground almonds
8–10 large slices of white or wholemeal
    (whole-wheat) bread

For the Calvados sauce
3 egg yolks
40g/1½oz/3 tbsp unrefined caster
    (superfine) sugar or rapadura
30ml/2 tbsp Calvados

1 Preheat the oven to 190°C/375°F/
Gas 5. Line the base of four individual
10cm/4in-diameter deep, earthenware
ramekin dishes with baking parchment.
Brush evenly and thoroughly with a little
of the melted butter or margarine, then
sprinkle each dish with a little of the
demerara sugar, rotating the dish in your
hands to coat each dish evenly.

VARIATIONS
• Slices of peeled pear or eating apples
can be used in this recipe instead of the
stoned, sliced plums.
• If you cannot find organic Calvados
any organic fruit-based spirit will work
in this dish.

2 Place the stoned plum slices in a pan
with the caster sugar, water and ground
cinnamon and cook gently for 5 minutes,
or until the plums have softened slightly.
Leave the plums to cool, then stir in
the ground almonds.

3 Cut the crusts off the bread and then
use a plain pastry cutter to cut out four
rounds to fit the bases of the ramekins.
Dip the bread rounds into the melted
butter and fit them into the dishes. Cut
four more rounds to fit the tops of the
dishes and set aside.

4 Cut the remaining bread into strips,
dip into the melted butter and use to
line the sides of the ramekins completely.

5 Divide the plum mixture among the
lined dishes and level the tops with the
back of a spoon. Place the bread rounds
on top and brush with the remaining
butter. Place the ramekins on a baking
sheet and bake for 25 minutes.

6 Make the sauce just before the
charlottes are ready. Place the egg yolks
and caster sugar in a large bowl, and
whisk them together until pale. Place the
bowl over a pan of simmering water and
whisk in the Calvados. Continue whisking
until the mixture is very light and frothy.

7 Remove the charlottes from the oven
and turn out on to warm serving plates.
Pour a little sauce over and around the
charlottes and serve immediately.

COOK'S TIP
For an extra creamy dessert, serve the
puddings with Greek (US strained plain)
yogurt or crème fraîche.

GARLIC MAYONNAISE

Fresh wet organic garlic is available in spring and summer, but try to use dried, cured bulbs as they have a more pungent flavour for this mouthwatering creamy mayonnaise.

SERVES FOUR TO SIX

2 large egg yolks
pinch of dried mustard
about 300ml/½ pint/1¼ cups mild olive oil
15–30ml/1–2 tbsp lemon juice, white wine
    vinegar or warm water
2–4 garlic cloves
sea salt and ground black pepper

1 Make sure the egg yolks and oil have come to room temperature before you start. Place the yolks in a bowl with the mustard and a pinch of salt, and whisk together to mix.

2 Gradually whisk in the oil, one drop at a time. When almost half the oil has been fully incorporated, start to add it in a slow, steady stream, whisking all the time.

3 As the mayonnaise starts to thicken, thin it down with a few drops of lemon juice or vinegar, or a few teaspoons of warm water.

4 When the mayonnaise is as thick as soft butter, stop adding oil. Season the mayonnaise to taste and add more lemon juice or vinegar as required.

5 Crush the garlic with the blade of a knife and stir it into the mayonnaise. For a slightly milder flavour, blanch the garlic twice in plenty of boiling water, then purée the cloves before beating them into the mayonnaise.

WATCHPOINT
The very young, the elderly, pregnant women and those in ill-health or with a compromised immune system are advised against consuming raw eggs or dishes containing them.

VARIATIONS
• To make Provençal aioli, crush 3–5 garlic cloves with a pinch of salt in a bowl, then whisk in the egg yolks. Omit the mustard but continue as above.
• For spicy garlic mayonnaise, omit the mustard and stir in 2.5ml/½ tsp harissa or red chilli paste and 5ml/1 tsp sun-dried tomato purée (paste) with the garlic.
• Use roasted garlic purée or puréed smoked garlic to create a different flavour.
• Beat in about 15g/½oz mixed fresh herbs such as tarragon, parsley, chervil and chives.

CONFIT of SLOW-COOKED ONIONS

This jam of caramelized onions will keep for several days in a sealed jar in the refrigerator.
You can use red, white or yellow onions, but yellow onions will give the sweetest result.

SERVES SIX TO EIGHT

30ml/2 tbsp olive oil
15g/½oz/1 tbsp butter or
    non-hydrogenated margarine
500g/1¼lb onions, sliced
3–5 fresh thyme sprigs
1 fresh bay leaf
30ml/2 tbsp unrefined light muscovado
    (brown) sugar or rapadura,
    plus a little extra
50g/2oz/¼ cup prunes, chopped
30ml/2 tbsp balsamic vinegar,
    plus a little extra
120ml/4fl oz/½ cup red wine
sea salt and ground black pepper

1 Reserve 5ml/1 tsp of the oil, then heat the rest with the butter in a small, heavy pan. Add the onions, cover and cook gently for 15 minutes, stirring occasionally.

2 Season with salt and plenty of pepper, then add the thyme, bay leaf and sugar. Cook slowly, uncovered, for another 15–20 minutes, or until the onions are very soft and dark.

3 Add the prunes, vinegar and wine with 60ml/4 tbsp water and cook over a low heat, stirring frequently, for a further 20 minutes, or until most of the liquid has evaporated. Add a little water and reduce the heat if the mixture dries too quickly.

4 Adjust the seasoning, adding more sugar and/or vinegar to taste. Leave the confit to cool, then stir in the remaining 5ml/1 tsp oil. The confit is best stored for 24 hours before eating. Serve either cold or warm.

VARIATION
Baby onions with tomato and orange
Gently fry 500g/1¼lb peeled pickling (pearl) onions or small *cipollini* in 60ml/ 4 tbsp olive oil until lightly browned, then sprinkle in 45ml/3 tbsp of unrefined soft light brown sugar or rapadura. Let the onions caramelize a little, then add 7.5ml/ 1½ tsp crushed coriander seeds, 250ml/ 8fl oz/1 cup red wine, 2 bay leaves, a few thyme sprigs, 3 strips orange zest and 45ml/3 tbsp tomato purée (paste) and the juice of 1 orange. Cook very gently, uncovered, for 1 hour, stirring occasionally until the sauce is thick and reduced. Uncover for the last 20 minutes of cooking time. Sharpen with 15–30ml/ 1–2 tbsp sherry vinegar and serve cold, sprinkled with chopped fresh parsley.

APPLE and TOMATO CHUTNEY

This mellow, golden, spicy chutney makes the most of fresh autumn produce. Any type of organic tomatoes can be used successfully in this recipe.

MAKES ABOUT 1.8KG/4LB

1.3kg/3lb cooking apples
1.3kg/3lb tomatoes
2 large onions
2 garlic cloves
250g/9oz/1¾ cups pitted dates
2 red (bell) peppers
3 dried red chillies
15ml/1 tbsp black peppercorns
4 cardamom pods
15ml/1 tbsp coriander seeds
10ml/2 tsp cumin seeds
10ml/2 tsp ground turmeric
5ml/1 tsp sea salt
600ml/1 pint/2½ cups distilled malt vinegar
1kg/2¼lb/5¼ cups unrefined granulated
    sugar or rapadura

3 Pour in the vinegar and sugar and then leave to simmer for 30 minutes, stirring occasionally. Add the red pepper and cook for a further 30 minutes, stirring more frequently as the chutney becomes thick and pulpy.

4 Spoon the chutney into warm, dry, sterilized jars. Seal each jar with a waxed circle and cover with a tightly fitting cellophane top. Leave to cool, then label and store in a cool, dry place.

1 Peel and chop the apples. Peel and chop the tomatoes, onions and garlic. Quarter the dates. Core and seed the peppers, then cut into chunky pieces. Put all the prepared ingredients, except the red peppers, into a preserving pan.

2 Slit the chillies. Put the peppercorns and remaining spices into a mortar and roughly crush with a pestle. Add the chillies, spices and salt to the pan.

FOCACCIA

This is a flattish bread, originating from Genoa in Italy, made with flour, olive oil and salt.
There are many variations from many regions but this is the traditional type.

MAKES 1 ROUND 25CM/10IN LOAF

25g/1oz fresh yeast
400g/14oz/3½ cups unbleached strong
 white bread flour
10ml/2 tsp sea salt
75ml/5 tbsp olive oil
10ml/2 tsp coarse sea salt

1 Dissolve the yeast in 120ml/4fl oz/
½ cup warm water. Allow to stand for
10 minutes. Sift the strong white bread
flour into a large bowl, make a well in
the centre, and add the yeast, salt and
30ml/2 tbsp oil. Mix in the flour and add
more water to make a dough.

2 Turn out on to a floured work surface
and knead the dough until smooth and
elastic. Return to the bowl, cover with a
cloth, and leave to rise in a warm place
for 2–2½ hours until doubled in bulk.

3 Knock back the dough and knead
again for a few minutes. Press into an
oiled 25cm/10in tart tin, and cover with
a damp cloth. Leave the dough to rise
again for 30 minutes.

4 Preheat the oven to 200°C/400°F/
Gas 6. Poke the dough all over with your
fingers, to make little dimples in the
surface. Pour the remaining oil over the
dough, using a pastry brush to take it to
the edges. Sprinkle with the salt.

5 Bake for 20–25 minutes, until the
bread is a pale gold. Carefully remove
from the tin and leave to cool on a rack.
The bread is best eaten on the same
day, but it also freezes very well.

VARIATIONS
Focaccia is often baked with a selection
of different toppings. Before baking, lightly
sprinkle over any or a combination of the
following: chopped pitted olives, slices of
red or yellow (bell) pepper, sprigs of fresh
rosemary or diced sun-dried tomatoes.

OLIVE BREAD

Variations of this strongly flavoured bread are popular all over the Mediterranean.
For this Greek recipe use rich, oily olives or those marinated with herbs.

MAKES TWO 675G/1½LB LOAVES

2 red onions, thinly sliced
30ml/2 tbsp olive oil
225g/8oz/2 cups pitted black
    or green olives
50g/2oz fresh yeast
800g/1¾lb/7 cups strong white bread flour
7.5ml/1½ tsp salt
45ml/3 tbsp each roughly chopped parsley,
    coriander (cilantro) and mint

1 Fry the onions in the oil until soft.
Roughly chop the olives.

2 Dissolve the yeast in 250ml/8fl oz/
1 cup warm water. Allow to stand for
10 minutes. Put the flour, salt and herbs
in a large bowl with the olives and fried
onions and add the yeast mixture.

3 Mix with a round-bladed knife, adding
as much warm water as is necessary to
make a soft dough.

4 Turn out on to a lightly floured surface
and knead for about 10 minutes. Put in a
clean bowl, cover with clear film (plastic
wrap) and leave in a warm place until
doubled in bulk.

5 Preheat the oven to 220°C/425°F/
Gas 7. Lightly grease two baking sheets.
Turn the dough on to a floured surface
and cut in half. Shape into two rounds and
place on the baking sheets. Cover the
dough loosely with lightly oiled clear film
and leave until doubled in size.

VARIATION
Shape the dough into 16 small rolls. Slash
the tops as in step 6 and reduce the
cooking time to 25 minutes.

6 Slash the tops of the loaves two or
three times with a knife, then bake for
about 40 minutes, or until the loaves
sound hollow when tapped on the
bottom. Transfer to a wire rack to cool.

CHAPATIS

More and more types of organic bread are available, but chapatis simply have to be made by hand. These chewy, unleavened breads are eaten throughout Northern India. They are usually served as an accompaniment to spicy dishes.

2 Knead for 5–6 minutes until smooth. Place in a lightly oiled bowl, cover with a damp dishtowel and leave to rest for 30 minutes. Turn out on to a floured surface. Divide the dough into six equal pieces. Shape each piece into a ball.

3 Press the dough into a larger round with the palm of your hand, then roll into a 13cm/5in round. Stack, layered between clear film (plastic wrap), to keep moist.

4 Heat a griddle or heavy frying pan over a medium heat for a few minutes until hot. Take one chapati, brush off any excess flour, and place on the griddle. Cook for 30–60 seconds, or until the top begins to bubble and white specks appear on the underside.

5 Turn the chapati over using a metal spatula and cook for a further 30 seconds. Remove from the pan and keep warm, layered between a folded dishtowel, while cooking the remaining chapatis. If you like, the chapatis can be brushed lightly with melted ghee or butter immediately after cooking. Serve warm.

MAKES SIX CHAPATIS

175g/6oz/1½ cups *atta* or wholemeal (whole-wheat) flour
2.5ml/½ tsp sea salt
120ml/4fl oz/about ½ cup water
5ml/1 tsp sunflower oil
melted ghee, butter or non-hydrogenated margarine, for brushing (optional)

COOK'S TIP

Atta or *ata* is a very fine wholemeal flour, which is only found in Indian stores and supermarkets. It is sometimes simply labelled chapati flour. *Atta* can also be used for making rotis and other Indian flat breads.

1 Sift the flour and salt into a large mixing bowl. Add the water and mix to a soft dough using your hand or a round-bladed knife. Knead in the oil, then turn the dough out on to a lightly floured surface.